I, Wayne Gretzky

I, Wayne Gretzky

I Wayne Gretzky

Short Stories by
Rob Gordon

For media inquiries, please contact Rob directly: e-mail r.gordon@cogeco.ca; at 905 337 9377

To order additional copies of this book, contact:
Xlibris Corporation
1-888-795-4274
www.Xlibris.com
Orders@Xlibris.com
107533

Table of Contents

Foreword

"Sitting in the class in SSM, Sir James Dunn High School, grade 11, staring out the window day after day at the many feet of piled snow, staring at the clock counting down the minutes to either that day's game or practice, I never knew for the life of me that Canada's number one world traveller was sitting directly beside me!

That's why my father always told me to take the time and see what is going on around you, get to know the people, well unfortunately I didn't get to know Rob Gordon.

Maybe had I not turned pro at 17 and moved on with my career, I would have had that one more year, 365 days to get to know the real Rob.

Well maybe by reading this book I will get to know him or at least maybe remember him!!"

99
Wayne Gretzky

Introduction

This is a story about an incredible opportunity, about chance, and about circumstance. This is a book about life and the humour that is found in the age-old practice of telling stories. In grade 11, the practice of seating people in alphabetical order led to the unique experience of sitting beside Wayne Gretzky in seven of eight classes at Sir James Dunn Collegiate and Vocational School in Sault Ste. Marie, Ontario, Canada. Although Wayne had hailed from Brantford, he had been drafted by the Soo Greyhounds of the Ontario Hockey League and was billeted in Sault Ste. Marie for a year. I knew Wayne as a classmate and acquaintance and had the chance to share a few interesting experiences with him. The most important of these was several days after he signed his first big professional contract with Nelson Skalbania, the owner of the WHA's Indianapolis Racers in 1978.

June 12, 1978 Front Page Sports – Globe and Mail;
used by permission Canadian Press

1

When Wayne returned from his whirlwind weekend, the news had just barely come out.

Wayne walked into geography class and sat down beside me with a smug smile. I said, "Holy cats! I didn't know you were that good. You are going to be very wealthy some day. Heck! You are very wealthy now!" It seemed natural at the time to politely ask for a piece of the action. So I did. "Hey, Wayne, surely there is some way I can capitalize on this, hey, how about I write a book about you?"

"That's a good idea," he said. I immediately turned away and drafted up a contract. "Sign this," I said. Without a second thought, Wayne signed the rights for me to write a book about him. I immediately had it witnessed by my two alphabetically close friends Don Elliot and Scott Forbes who sat on the other side of me.

Wayne Gretzky's first professional autograph, June 13, 1978.

Wayne and I spent a good part of the class discussing the contents. Wayne mentioned his father had a shoebox full of photos that he could have him send up and that there would be lots to write about. It's hard to believe that boredom set in, and we started paying attention to what the teacher (Mrs. Morrow) was talking about. I left the class with my autograph, took it home, and put it in an envelope marked Do Not Throw Out, which was a warning for my mother, who liked cleaning out my stuff. I then forgot about it. My aspirations as a writer and that piece of paper wouldn't come together for more than seven years.

Two other significant incidents from my association with Wayne and that period in high school stand out in my mind. Earlier that year, 1978, while sitting in geography class, I had made a bet with Wayne for two dollars on the Stanley Cup. Although Montreal was my favorite team, Wayne convinced me that I should take the rest of the league instead so that he could bet on Montreal. When the 1977–78 season ended, I was happy that the Canadians, coached by Scotty Bowman, had won the Stanley Cup, beating the Boston Bruins in the finals, four games to two. The two-dollar loss to Wayne Gretzky was fairly easy to take, and to make it more memorable, I made a point to pay him with an envelope full of pennies. One other memory from those days was from physics class. Our teacher, Mr. Austeberry, used to post a chart after every weekly quiz with our names beside the marks we had obtained out of twenty. I was often near the top and Wayne was often near the bottom. Of course, there is no moral in this. Physics has a huge bearing on most things that we do as humans, including the bounce of a puck. At the end of the day, I chose to study geophysics and recall getting a few low marks myself along the way.

Unfortunately, Wayne wasn't around very much over that school year, so despite conversations, by the lockers or when walking between classes and other musings in class, I didn't really get to know him that well. However, I do recall joking around a lot in geography class. So I put my contract away with not much of a realization of how unique a piece of paper it might become one day. I wasn't to actually see Mr. Gretzky again for seven years.

Just after I graduated from Queen's University with my engineering degree in 1985, while watching the Edmonton Oilers and Wayne Gretzky win their second straight Stanley cup in 1984–85, dollar signs flashed in front of my eyes as I thought of my book contract and how it would lead to my infinite wealth. The story of the man who uncovered the singing frog in the Bugs Bunny sketch comes to mind as an analogy. So, right then, I decided to write a book.

Scott Forbes
Greg Funk
Kristel Gibb
Judi Gilbert
Paul Glassford
Frank Glover
Kelly Godson

Rob Gordon
Michael Grbich
Veronica Greco
Wayne Gretsky
Debbie Hall
Beth Harry
Elizabeth Hart

Laurie Haysey
Cynthia Hazell
Cheryl Hernden
Colleen Hewett
Kathy Hodgson
Shauna Holmes
Jamie Horbatuk

Janet Horne
David Hugill
Linda Hurdie
Kay Ingram
Karen Ireland
San Ireland
Heather Irwin

Ginny Jackson
Shari Jackson
Michael Jones
William Katerenchuk
Robert Kennedy
Nancy Killoran
Allan Killoran

Grade 11 class photo (1978) Sir James Dunn High School, Sault Ste. Marie, Ontario.

So the catalyst for this book was the story of obtaining, arguably, one of the most significant autographs of our time, but this incredible story really just ties into a series of events and tales that make up my life and travels. While I was growing up, several, or should I say a lot of, unique events and adventures happened to me. Whenever I recounted these tales, people have laughed. I felt that if people smiled and laughed at the stories I told about these adventures, then perhaps I should write them down.

I slowly, over time, kept jotting down stories and notes, but as life carries on, you realize every day is a piece of a new story and it is hard to keep up. The book became a work in progress. Then in 2002, I decided to go back to school to broaden my horizons. A second catalyst occurred during a marketing class where I happened to arrive a minute late and was forced to grab a desk at the front of the class. My marketing professor, Ken Hardy from the IVEY School of Business, walked in the class right behind me and said, "We need someone to get the class going, it's early and we need to get woken up. Can someone get up and tell a joke or a story?" I looked up and scoffed. I thought to myself, *What idiot would get up in front of the class and tell a joke.* Then, like a nightmare come true, from the back of the class someone said, "Get Rob Gordon to tell the story of how he found his watch." The story was familiar. I had told it to a group of students from the other class the night before at the local tavern, and one from that crowd had slipped into our class that day. I melted, and the next thing I knew after several chants from the class like the sounds the head hunting natives made while taking Abbot and Costello to the big pot for a boiling hot dinner, Mr. Hardy was pulling me forward. So there I was getting some firsthand experience at public speaking. Following a terrifying start, the story started to flow, and soon, the class was in an uproar.

The next week I came to class and a colleague said, "What are you going to tell us today?" I wondered what he was talking about as he pointed to the front board, and there in the agenda was 8:00–8:15—Rob Gordon's story time! Each week, they forced me to tell another story. By the time the course was over, not only had my ability to speak in public improved greatly, but I was also motivated to finally write some of these ridiculous stories down. Thus completing this book with stories so far.

So one of my favorite crowd-pleasing stories, "The Wayne Gretzky Story," has somehow evolved into this book of short stories. I believe many readers will be able to relate to some of these growing up and life experience stories. Through these stories, perhaps you can bring back some of your own.

A Good Place to Come From

In 1974, Morley Torgov wrote a memorable book called *A Good Place to Come From*. It recounted stories and scenes that were known to be landmarks from Sault Ste. Marie and won the Stephen Leacock Memorial Medal for Humor. My parents moved to Sault Ste. Marie in 1961, and in 1962, I was born. As a child, everything seemed so big: the houses, the trees, and the snowbanks. The first chapter of this book relates to early years and recounts "mammoth adventures and tales of small people." My memories of my younger life have always been very vivid, and I have always claimed to have a good memory, and so I attempt to tell these stories as they are remembered. These stories have been told repeatedly to friends, relatives, and unsuspecting strangers and provide a glimpse into some mischievous developing years for me. Fortunately or unfortunately, some antics of mine are not put on paper.

Introducing Little Johnny Luxton and Snowball Season

As a child, my best friend and, almost daily, my worst enemy was little Johnny Luxton. For many years, we took turns growing up and beating up each other. As five-year-olds, we would start the day as friends and wind up throwing stones at each other. It was a frequent sight to see me running home crying after little Johnny had ploughed me one in the stomach. All of the mothers on the block hated little Johnny Luxton. John was always doing something wrong. As a child, he was mostly known for stone throwing, hitting people and running, breaking windows and, above all, stealing. John was so bad at the latter that a familiar scene was his mother at the front door with

Little John Luxton with me. John has taken my ball (1969).

a screaming little Johnny in tow and a wheelbarrow full of children's toys, asking if any of them belonged at our house. That wheelbarrow was always full of the neatest stuff. Johnny was a key character in my early days and had an influence on the outcome of many a day as you shall see.

I distinctly remember Saturday mornings in the winter. Johnny and I would head off to the plaza. Often, older kids would grab the both of us and threaten to pummel us with snowballs for something Johnny had done to a little brother or sister months or even years before. In most cases, I was lucky, and they would release me. From a safe distance, I could hear and see poor old Johnny getting pummelled by snowballs after the bigger kids would say,

"We'll give you the count of two to run." John, realizing the hopelessness of it all, would sometimes never run.

One winter's day, John and I began a relentless, vicious snowball attack on John's neighbor's front window. Despite repeated warnings to stop, we continued to throw snowballs from behind the four-foot snowbank. "I know who you are!" Mr. Shaw would yell. We continued our attack for twenty minutes with no response until "I have your hockey sticks! Now stop or you'll never get them back!" It was hard to believe he had snuck out the back door, waded through snow, gone into John's garage, and pinched our sticks. A verbal truce was quickly agreed upon, and two seven-year-olds left with our heads down.

A favorite sport of John's and mine was hiding behind hedges or between houses and throwing snowballs point-blank into car windows as they sped by.

My seventh birthday (1969). Note little Johnny,
a mean little Indian with a "fierce grin."

Once, just after we sent the snowballs flying, a car slid to a stop before being hit by the snowballs. We were stunned. Finally, we started to run. It was not our lucky day; it turned out to be the police commissioner's car, and we were promptly caught. He drove me home in the police cruiser and spent some time giving grief to my dad. That time, John escaped. However, on another occasion, Johnny and I coerced another friend named Glen Macdonald to join us. We proceeded to hide between a couple of houses off Shannon Road. John had a deadly aim, and with one thirty-foot bullet of a shot, he loosened the hubcap of a souped-up Chevy van. How we laughed. Suddenly, the van slid to a halt, and three big guys jumped out and yelled, "Hey, you!" John, Glen Macdonald, and I started to run. John and I left Glen far behind. We knew only too well what we might be in for. We ran down the dark street that cut the crescent. I cut left, following John down a driveway. Johnny was a very fast runner. I knew I couldn't keep up. The van was now at the mouth of the driveway. John ran into the yard and over the fence into the open park. I nipped along the back of the house and dove behind some pails. I peeked out moments later to see two huge boys jump over the fence and promptly catch John in the park. An uncontrollable smile crossed my face as I heard John's screams, which became muffled as his head was buried in the deep snow. The next day, Glen recounted how he had been caught first but escaped harm by saying, "It was John Luxton and Rob Gordon who did it."

By the time high school rolled around, John and I hadn't changed very much. We used to throw snowballs at the street lamps on the way to and from school. One day, outside the reverend's house, John hit the lamp. This time, it fell loose and crashed to the ground. I looked around and saw the reverend's wife peering out of the window. I suggested that we go and tell her it was cracked anyway, and we were just knocking it down to prevent it from falling on her kids. We approached the door. When the lady came to the door, Johnny did the talking. John tried to explain things, but right away, I knew she hadn't seen anything. I knew the best thing was to just leave her confused, and so we left her there with an astonished look on her face as I dragged John away.

The Snowball Area

Wintertime in the "Sault" meant piles of fun. There was always plenty of snow. The snowbanks seemed to be ten feet high. Every day was a giant adventure as we trudged to school in the morning, home for a quick lunch, and back again for the afternoon. My memory is much like the recent advertisement of Tim Horton's where the child is buried in huge mounds of snow and walking to school in blizzards. Our school was named East View Public School and was about a fifteen-minute walk. When we got to school, the first thing we would do was to run to the "snowball area." This was a large area in the back of the schoolyard near the pond where anything went. The only thing missing were the signs that said "Enter at Your Own Risk." The area was far enough away from the school to keep stray snowballs from flying through the windows. It was in the snowball area where the history of the west was replayed daily.

East View had First Nations children that lived near the city on the Garden River Reservation. Two or three buses arrived daily with a wild bunch of raucous fellows and a quiet group of shy girls. The white boys and the First Nations fought to gain control of a large hill in the middle of the snowball area. Here, there were always more whites, but the Indians always seemed much bigger. Getting thrown down the hill was just part of the whole game. We always came in from recess soaking wet.

I recently talked to Steve Bodnar, another high school chum and an old friend of Wayne's, now the principal of East View, and he mentioned that the snowball area disappeared long before his time.

The Snowplow Story

Well into high school, John and I found other winter activities to create enjoyment in the wintertime. Faithfully, on a Friday night, we would head off for adventure in Johnny's mother's Volkswagen Beetle. We would derive great pleasure from simply ploughing the snowbanks with her car. The famous plate undercarriage of the Beetle made us nearly indestructible.

If we had three people in the car, I would often roll down the passenger side window as we were ploughing down the road. Snow would just billow into the back, covering any unsuspecting friend in the backseat.

One evening, we were driving quickly down the road back from a friend's house. I indicated to John to start ploughing the snowbanks. At this point, he drove at right angles to the road, up and over the small bank and across a huge front yard. We then completely leveled a gigantic snow fort and drove out of the driveway. "Ho! Ho! Merry Christmas," we yelled and laughed our heads off as we sped away. We drove a few blocks away and parked in a friend's driveway to brush off the snow. We were still laughing when a big 4×4 truck pulled up and stopped

Plowing the roads with Johnny's mothers volkswagon.

at the end of the driveway. It looked like it was intentionally blocking our way. I dove into the backseat and locked the doors as a huge man stomped up the driveway. His voice bellowed loud four-letter words. He walked up to John and punched him in the chest. I cringed. He screamed and yelled and punched John again. John had no excuse. To save himself, John volunteered to shovel the guy's driveway for a few days. Later that night, we apologized profusely as he opened his garage door, handed us some shovels, and said, "Shut up and dig!"

Introducing Little Billy Goodall

An addition to the neighborhood in the early '70s was the Goodall family. This family consisted of a single mother, a daughter, and two brothers: Kevin and Billy. Billy happened to be my age, around ten years old, and so we quickly became friends. I have trouble remembering too much about Billy other than we used to play one-on-one street hockey for hours and hours after school. Billy was a very quiet and polite boy, but he did have a mischievous side. As we grew up, we grew apart, and finally, he moved to a house up on the hill. Bill, like most of my friends, didn't get along well with John Luxton, and so when I was playing with Billy, John was usually nowhere around. We still got in trouble a fair bit, so maybe it wasn't just Johnny who was the common denominator with trouble. Maybe it was Billy?

Well many years later, in 1989, at one Christmas Eve party held by our neighbors, the Sagles, we were exchanging stories in the kitchen. Cathy Sagle had been a former babysitter in the days of Billy Goodall and was now telling people what a wild kid I was to anyone who would listen including several other neighbors and her relatives. I tried to deny this, but Cathy, who was now an established audiologist, seemed to have quite a bit more credibility than a young engineer. Cathy recounted a story, which I had completely forgotten. Apparently, one Friday night, my parents were out. Cathy Sagle was babysitting and I was in my room. Looking out of the window, I saw little Billy Goodall across the street with a hockey stick and ball. I opened the window and whistled for him to come over. Billy was supposed to be home babysitting his little sister but had left her watching TV and wanted to play hockey. I said that I had to stay in, but we could make fudge at my house instead. I helped Billy crawl up in my window. Cathy was doing her homework at the kitchen table down the hall. Billy and I devised a plan. I walked out to the kitchen and asked Cathy if she wanted to see my new fish. Once inside the door, Billy jumped on her back and I grabbed her legs. Soon, she was on the floor squealing like a pig. I held her face down as Billy, behaving like one of Ian Tyson's buckaroos, quickly lashed her feet and hands. To stop her screams, we rammed a sock in her mouth. She was still quite loud, so we had to drag her down the stairs and shut her in the basement. We turned on the TV for her and ran upstairs. With newfound freedom, we put on a couple of my brother's Edgar Winter records full blast, got out my mother's recipe book, and started to make fudge. After a while, we decided to go downstairs to the basement. Cathy, who had been quietly lying on her side watching TV, started squirming. It was obvious from her tears that she was somewhat distressed. We took the rag out of her mouth, and she pleaded for us to untie her because she was losing circulation in her hands. We complied. She was now screaming and kicking. I ran up the stairs and Billy was close behind. Suddenly, I heard Billy yelp. He was being dragged down the stairs by an uncontrollable monster. I watched as Billy was beaten at the bottom of the stairs. Next, Billy was dragged up the stairs, through the house, and thrown out of my window. Landing on his head, he was heard screaming while running home. I was confined to my room. Cathy never told on us until the story was recounted at that Christmas Eve party in 1989.

Little Robbie Gordon

Steve Smylie and the Free Haircuts

At public school, my best friend was Steve Smylie. Steve was a short, tough kid with large teeth and a big smile. One of my first elaborate life experiences with Steve, which I recall, was an incident that happened at afternoon recess in kindergarten. Afternoon recess at the kindergarten level was established as a rest period for the teacher. Surprisingly enough, the standard practice was for the teacher to leave all the kids alone for twenty to thirty minutes. The normal practice was to get your own towel from the cupboard and place it beside your desk, lie down, make no noise, and take a nap. I still remember the red-and-green Scottish plaid of my towel. Oh, how hard the floor was.

Generally, most of the class quietly lay down and behaved while the teacher left to share a moment with her colleagues in the teacher's room. Sometimes, whispering would be heard between students. As in most classes, there were always a couple of troublemakers.

Steve and I were up playing tag as soon as the teacher left the room. We ran through the obstacle course at full speed, jumping over the lumps on the floor, occasionally stepping on a leg or an arm by mistake. Soon, several kids said they were going to tell on us. This could obviously create problems and something had to be done. I grabbed a couple of pairs of the little metal paper scissors that are common to kindergarten classes and gave one to Steve. After we dealt with the squealers, we snuck around the class on tiptoes, chopping huge clumps of hair from our napping, unsuspecting victims.

Screams soon filled the air as we raced around like two housewives on a shopping spree, trying to cut as many heads as possible. Soon, the teacher, Mrs. Kemp, was back. She was in shock and then anger came over her like a tsunami hit. She started screaming as dozens of kids were bawling. Quickly, she zeroed in on us, and soon, Steve and I were crying as we were promptly hauled out of the class, being swatted, and beaten on our way to the principal's office.

One of our victims was named David Brideaux. David had been close-cropped, almost scalped, and the massive clump of hair that had been removed was so large that, to this day, he still has a ducktail sticking out the front of his forehead.

Steve and I were best of friends through grade four and then we went our separate ways. I recently saw him at a high school reunion. After all those years, he said, "Remember that time . . ."

From my 1970 grade 2 storybook. The teacher's comment about Steve is circled.

Steve Smylie Meets Little Johnny Luxton

One day, Steve and I were walking home from school. Upon approaching my house, John Luxton appeared from behind the bushes. John wanted to know where we were going. I said, "To my house, to have some milk." At that point, a flash of jealousy crossed John's face. He bent over and picked up a large rock and threw it. Before we could react, the rock struck Steve Smylie square in the mouth. Broken teeth and blood oozed from Steve's mouth as he started to scream. John ran. I ran after him and Steve ran home screaming. The scream brought neighbors to their doors for blocks around.

Steve's large, big teeth were never the same. To this day, Steve Smylie has hated John Luxton. John fails to recall the incident despite the fact that these sorts of things were regular, almost daily, occurrences in the quiet neighborhood. Once, John pulled a similar stunt on a little fellow named Jeffery Rockburn. This time, in front of several mothers, he threw a gigantic rock and hit Jeffery Rockburn right in the forehead. Blood streamed down little Jeffery's face as the mothers collectively chased John home. Smylie and Rockburn were just a few characters that roamed the local block. It was amusing to reflect on their names and how John's actions influenced them so literally.

Steve Smylie and I Meet Big Paul Lewis

The street behind ours was called Lewis Road named after the contractor who built most of the houses on that street. One day, while walking up the street with Steve, we noticed Big Paul Lewis standing in front of us. Paul was at least one year older, about one foot taller, and he could easily kill either one of us. If we were ever referred to as bullies, then Big Paul was a super bully. I remember Paul as a fellow that was always threatening.

"No one passes in front of my house without paying," he yelled. This was like "live" Billy Goats Gruff meeting the troll. Steve and I were terrified. As Big Paul came closer, we got closer together. I told Steve we were either going to have to split up and run, or both attack him and we might have a chance. Initially, we tried to scoot around him, but he came charging at us. We both turned and pounced. Big Paul wasn't expecting that. Fists were flying. Soon, the three of us were rolling on the ground in front of McPhail's house, which sat on the corner of the crescent. After a frightful fight that seemed to last forever, it became obvious that we had the upper hand. Paul was starting to blubber.

The McPhails owned a tiny poodle that had pooped all over their lawn. It was late fall, so things were cold. Peculiar to this type of poodle was that the entire poop was white, and most of it was hard. With Steve holding Paul down and telling him never to bother us again, in our moment of glory, I grabbed a hunk of poop that was nearby and rammed it in Big Paul's mouth. He started screaming so loud that his big sister came running. Steve and I took off. She swore she would kill us. For two weeks, Steve and I had to sneak home from school as a herd of grade 8s chased us relentlessly.

One day, we split up, and by the time we met up again, Steve was soaked in muddy water from head to toe, cursing me and saying I had better watch out because I was going to get it worse. I was never caught. Paul continued to be a very threatening figure in the neighborhood, especially when I was alone. To this day, I always look over my shoulder when I pass by Lewis Road.

Just a Sweet Tooth!

One of the problems faced by a parent is making sure their children do not take a liking to stealing. As a child, I was jealous of all the things Johnny Luxton had. I am not sure at which point in time I developed a bad case of sticky fingers..My habits got me into several bouts of trouble. I had a wild desire for candy and lots of it. This turned out to be a bad thing. Sault Ste. Marie was one of those communities that fought to keep fluoride out of the water. I used to go to the dentist and come home with just one cavity just like the Crest ads said. The problem arose because I went to the dentist twenty to thirty times as a child. So before I was six, all my teeth fell out.

To placate my wild desires for candy, I needed money. There were several sources, but my ten-cent-a-week allowance did not cut it. I would sneak into my mother's room and take a few nickels out of her purse to supplement my allowance. A trip to Sing Hongs confectionary on the way to afternoon school would fill my pockets with Bazooka Joe gum, some hockey cards, and sometimes a chocolate bar. The local First Nation children at the school knew me as one who had gum, so I was targeted to go to the store for them as they were not allowed to go to the store. Or I was targeted to hand over some gum. They used to wait at the edge of the school and repeat an old war cry, "Gimmie gum. Gimmie gum." Not obliging meant a run-for-your-life scenario, the end result being thrown in the mud and having all gum stripped away. As I now required huge amounts of gum to satisfy the whole native population at East View Public School, naturally I needed more money. I started taking quarters from my mother's purse, leaving the nickels and dimes. It was very frustrating when there were no quarters in her purse, so I began to look for other sources.

One day, I opened my father's desk drawer. There wrapped in some Kleenex were what appeared to be a hundred quarters. At first, I took just one or two, but soon, I was taking three or four. After all, I could get two chocolate bars, three Tootsie Rolls, and four packs of gum for seventy cents. As his roll of quarters shrunk away, I started searching for another source, and sure enough, I found one. My brother kept his paper-route money in a small drawer in his desk. One day, I took $3 in bills. I was rich, and it was so easy. I went straight to the IGA store and bought $3 worth of junk food: five Tootsie Rolls, five packs of Chiclets, licorice, chips, corn puffs, and ten huge jawbreakers. I started eating right away. It was four o'clock and supper was at six. After stuffing my face, I realized that I had had too much to eat and that I would have to get rid of the stuff before I got home. It was almost a whole grocery bag full of candy that I was carrying. I stopped at Johnny Luxton's house on the way home and attempted to give him five packs of Chiclets. His dad came to the door and looked perplexed. He said that John didn't want them. As I slowly walked up the street, I was being overcome with desperation. I threw all of the jawbreakers down the hill. The next thing I knew, Tom Sagle, my neighbor, appeared. Tom was a year older than me, and surely, he could help. What luck! "Hey, Tom, want some candy?" Tom's eyes lit up. "Sure," he said. "Okay, here you go," I said. Giving him the whole big grocery bag, I turned and walked home with a satisfied smile.

Dinner was fine. I was playing with my unwanted brussels sprouts and dreaming of Oh Henry! bars when suddenly there was a knock at the door. I ran behind my mother to see who it was. To my surprise, it was Mrs. Sagle from next door with a very familiar-looking bag of groceries. "Thank Robbie very much for this, but it's much too much for Tom," she said. My mother peered into the bag; a puzzled look crossed her face. I nipped back to the table and started eating my brussels sprouts. When my mother returned to the table, she had a rather stern look on her face. "Where did this come from?" she said.

Meanwhile, my brother had left the table quietly. He knew something was up. The next thing I knew, he had reappeared and was yelling, "Three dollars of my paper-route money is missing!" A short time later, I found myself alone in the car with my father. He was quietly asking what had happened that day and if I knew anything about the strange things that had happened. Of course, I denied everything. Finally, my father said, "I will now drive home, and if you don't speak up by the time we get to the driveway, I will lose it!" I knew the gig was up. As we pulled up our driveway, I was confessing to everything, much like the Classic Trinity Western, where the Mexican bandit says, "Emeliano tell everything" when the pistol is pointed up his nose!

I became the new paperboy on the block. I could barely lift the bag of papers. It was three weeks of torture. I took over my brother's route of Saturday *Toronto Star* papers. There were only eleven papers, but they were so thick, and you can imagine that the eleven subscribers were found over hell's half acre. Then something else occurred. My dad suddenly noticed something. His roll of quarters was diminished. Naturally, I was blamed. About sixty quarters were gone. Punishment was washing dishes at twenty-five cents an hour. It turned out that my dad had been collecting the silver 1967 special edition quarters with the cougar on them for quite some time. Needless to say, I am still washing dishes when I go home to visit as the price of those quarters has jumped substantially.

About ten years later, my dad had forgotten where he had hidden some 1976 Montreal Olympic coins. He came knocking after dinner one night and was thoroughly convinced that I had taken them. I was almost kicked out of the family for that incident. About a week later, he found them and I was cleared.

The gang (1975): Rob Gordon, Dwayne Maki, Gaston Lillieve, Tom Sagle, Bruce Maki, Steve Smylie, and Billy Goodall. Absent Johnny Luxton.

Giants amongst Us

Two of the First Nations kids that used to be a part of the Indian wars in the snowball area eventually went on to quite storied careers in Canadian sport. Both of these fellows turned into very talented professional athletes. One of the daily "kings of the castle" from the snowball area was a tall First Nation boy named Ted Nolan. Ted was in grade 6 when I was in grade 2. I did not get to know him other than feeling the pain as he whipped me down the hill.

Ted Nolan went on to play hockey and briefly played with Wayne Gretzky on the Greyhounds in 1978 before moving on to become a defenseman in the NHL with the Detroit Red Wings. I followed his career a bit and was quite proud to find out that he had coached the Greyhounds, and after leading them to three consecutive Memorial Cup finals, he finally succeeded in leading the team to a championship in front of the hometown crowd. These demonstrations of talent eventually led to a post as an assistant coaching job in the NHL for the Hartford Whalers. Subsequently, he was named head coach of the Buffalo Sabres where he won the Jack Adams Trophy for coach of the year in 1996. His story is quite well-known as he later left the Sabres after being offered just a one-year contract. He could not find work in the NHL for over five years, and it was rumored that he had been blackballed from the league by an old boy's network of managers. Other thoughts were that it was racial prejudice. I knew that he was talented enough that he would eventually return. Ted Nolan coached the New York Islanders in 2007 and 2008 and, more recently, the National Latvian Hockey Team. I always thought if Ken Dryden had hired him when he was running Toronto, the Leafs might have had a chance.

Ted Nolan graduation class 1973

The other boy was named Darren Zack. He was in my class. I think he was a year older because he was a giant of a boy. Darren, as evident from the picture, was bigger than the teacher, and he was untouchable in terms of class strength. Darren generally hung around a group of friends he had from the reserve but was also quite active at soccer and baseball. He was very good at threatening and scaring the likes of smaller people like me.

1975, East View Public School, grade 8. Darren Zack on the left, I am fifth from the left on the top row.

One year, we played on the same team in the house league soccer, and in one particular game, three of us were suspended for some reason (I can't remember what I did, but I believe I was just in the wrong place at the wrong time). We were banned from outdoor recess for one week. During that time, Darren used to force me to play a game with him where you put your hand on the desk, spread your fingers, and jab the table with a knife (his), trying to miss your opponent's fingers. Darren, after doing this to me at incredible speeds, would hand the knife over and demand that I do this to him. He would tell me that if I missed and cut him, he would kill me. He would also tell me to do it as fast as he did or he'd kill me. Needless to say, I am not really here today.

After this strange initial bonding period, another incident arose. Darren happened to be the last person to say his oral. He had made up all kinds of excuses, attempting to avoid the orations. One day, the teacher Mr. Cookman, who was almost as big as Darren, demanded that he say his oral that day after recess. I was merrily on my way to the baseball field when a giant hand grabbed me and hauled me back into the classroom. The teacher asked what was going on and Darren said, "Rob is going to help me with my oral."

"Is that so?" queried the teacher. With Darren's giant fingers slowly separating my arm, I said, "Sure." Darren was pleased and I heard the story of how he and some friends had gone squirrel hunting the previous weekend. After every sentence, he would ask me how it sounded. I enthusiastically said it was great. After recess, Darren actually managed to tell the whole class his story. The story was very funny, and the class roared with laughter. He got quite a good mark.

Many of our childhood friends and acquaintances go out in the wide world and are never heard from again. Although I haven't seen Darren in years, my father has clipped articles out of the local papers that have followed Darren's remarkable career as a champion softball pitcher.

Good as gold: Zack pitches in as Canada wins Pan Am softball crown

Canadian softball pitcher Darren Zack with a stack of softballs at the
PAN AM games Winnipeg, August 1st, 1999 Photo by John Lehman,
© National Post. Headline used by permission, Sault This Week.

There are so many adventures to tell from the early years. Tales that are fondly remembered from time to time, tales that set the stage and lay the groundwork for the development of a person. My first big Valentine, the dance, somehow managing to get the strap in grade 2, having my head smashed and teeth broken by a goalie stick in grade 6, and then into the next phase, high school. It was so much fun growing up in Sault Ste. Marie and, you know, the snowbanks were always over six feet high, and just like in the Tim Horton ads, we walked fifteen minutes home through blizzards for hot soup every day. I still tell Johnny Luxton stories every year, and my father, who is eighty, always perks up to recount the story of John and Tom Sagle breaking into our house one summer when we were away. "A startled house sitter caught them in Rob's room breaking his toys," much to the groans of all who have heard it a hundred times before.

John has settled down and is married with two great looking kids living in Ottawa.

Grade 8 ice sculpture. From left to right: Dave Wallace,
Rob Gordon, Dave Ferguson, and Doug Murray.

Of Brothers and Dogs
My Brother and I

Growing up with an older brother wasn't really that bad. My brother's name was Andrew and because he was seven years older, there never really was any competition. When there was, I was always squashed like a rebel uprising. My brother loves recalling how he tried to kill me when I was just a baby by holding a hand over my mouth and plugging my nose. For the most part though, I remember only vague memories of growing up with an older brother. As we got a bit older of course, we used to argue over possessions, and sometimes, these arguments would end in tears, mostly mine.

One of the first times that I remember truly relating to my brother was following first term exams at Christmas during my first year of university. Perhaps, we finally had common ground. We have related fairly well ever since, barring a few extraordinary stories that arose.

A Truck Door

One year I decided to write a Christmas letter for friends and relations. Initially, it was just to inform them of what I had been up to, but several circumstances that had arisen from dealings gone badly with my brother seemed to warrant some communication as I was looking for moral support. The following is my 1989 Christmas letter:

> Dear everyone:
>
> Merry Christmas, and good wishes for the New Year. I've done quite a lot of traveling this past year with the new job. I've gained some experience and have seen a few places. I have never liked this type of sums-me-up letter, but with Christmas rapidly approaching and no cards in the works, I figured this was my best bet. So if I can, I'd thought I would tell a Christmas story.
>
> Once upon a time, I had a nice brother. Andrew was his name. Andrew grew up with a seven-year age difference in his favor. I was the brunt of many of his tormenting beatings. As we grew older, nothing seemed to change. I was still the brunt of many of his tormenting beatings. One Christmas, things changed. I absolutely pounded him. Actually, I should clarify that. Andrew had come home from some faraway place three days before Christmas. On Christmas Eve, just before lunch, we were handed a huge list of very important tasks to do: go to the liquor store, drop off the gifts, pick up the gifts, do this do that. Andrew and I walked outside, looked at each other with glum looks, and then Andrew said, "Let's go to the Caswell for a couple." I had just returned from my

first term at Queen's and realized that now my brother was finally respecting me, only because we could share some time together at a bar! By six o'clock, we arrived home, a little tipsy. From that point on, we had a certain underlying bond. We were the Gordon boys. Christmas day arrived, and Andrew decided to get the old table hockey set out and challenged me to a game. Little did he know that I had become Champion of the Universe down at Queen's. I had annihilated some of the best tabletop hockey players around. Soon, we were in the living room in the midst of what was to become Rob's rout. Andrew came close with a good goal late in the third period, but the final score told all: 10–1. He had been pounded! I remained Champion of the Universe.

Time passed, we grew older, and several major events happened in our lives that affected both of us. But we were still the Gordon Boys. One Christmas, many years later, we were visiting at my Uncle Bob's cottage near Lake Boshkung. (Bob was what we refer to as a Scottish uncle, he was a very good childhood friend of my dad's. Bob is Robert Bateman, Canadian wildlife artist and conservationist.) My father, who had been making several major adjustments on the home front since my mom's passing, was using the occasion to introduce a lady to the family—Linda Savory.

There was a plan for everyone to go for a walk in the snow the day before New Year's. Andrew and I decided to duck out to the local hotel for a couple of drafts just before the big crowd got going. We jumped in his truck, and he proceeded to back up. His window was fogged up, so I opened my door a bit to see and give directions; he was going to end up in the bank, so I said, "Slow down and to the left." He turned more toward the bank and sped up. I yelled, "Stop," as the bank reached out and grabbed the passenger door and crumpled it into a little ball. Then there was silence.

Andrew looked over at me with a stunned look and immediately jumped out of his truck. I jumped out too. He looked at the door. Then out of the quiet, the entourage of binocular toting bird watching morning walkers came over the crest of the hill. "You fucking idiot," he yelled. "You are the idiot," I yelled. Many expletives were thrown back and forth at full volume.

The hikers passed quietly listening to the two chickadees. The air was soon filled with winter sounds as our voices died off. Linda, Alan, Birgit, and Uncle Bob with a bunch of kids, aunts, and uncles looked on. The silence was broken by another outburst of woodpeckers. "You (*&*&^&$$#@@! %##*(_8(**^%$&9^%709!!!!!"

I stormed off grabbed a checkbook and wrote the jerk a cheque for $300. "Here, this is to shut you up!"

"Thanks," he said. "Merry Christmas to you too!"

Our quarrel had ended for now. His door remained broken for some time; finally, I heard he got one for $70 at the junkyard and had used the rest of the cash to paint his truck and take his buddies and one of his many girlfriends to the pub for a few. Needless to say, I was quite agitated by all this. I should have never written that check. A few years passed during which time I fruitlessly attempted to get a rebate.

Andrew was tight with his money, and it would be hard to get that money out of him. I would have to think of a roundabout means to get even. I am still working on it.

Andrew Gordon, his truck, Flashman, and Rob driving home from Queen's on the back roads of Sylvan valley somewhere east of Sault St. Marie, spring 1985.

The Chair Story

It wasn't until a few years after that I was to visit him at his old schoolhouse out in the country. Andrew was having a big Christmas party and had invited friends from all over. For some reason, I was on his list. His good buddy Jock Irons was visiting from Alaska, and a bunch of faculty members from the University of Guelph were coming out to Orton for the party. It was going to be a big bash.

With the Christmas snow lying all around and the owls softly hooting in the cornfields, the mood was just right for a great evening. Neil Hughes, a buddy from school, had come over for the weekend and Andrew was particularly happy because he now had a couple of elves to do a multitude of chores around his home. After hauling wood around for most of the day, Neil and I shifted into the relaxed mode and started to pound back a few beers. People had arrived and music and booze flowed through the evening.

Around midnight, I went outside and brought Neil to show him something I had found in Andrew's garage. There in front of us was a very interesting item. It was a fan belt. This fan belt was a giant one, about six feet long. Looking farther, we noticed another interesting item. Over behind the woodpile was an old beaten-up leather rocking chair in very pathetic shape. Neil and I looked at each other with engineering smiles. We grabbed the belt and the chair and headed out to the road, which was smoothly snow covered and freshly ploughed. Backing up Neil's car, we attached the fan belt to the trailer hitch and then Neil jumped into the chair and attempted to look like a professional snow chairer.

Unfortunately, when the car moved forward, the chair would rock forward and the person would immediately fall out. We decided to change the configuration a bit. I became the guinea pig and stood on the runners, which protruded from the back of the chair and grabbed the reins. "OK, GO!" In a minute, Neil was speeding down the road. "Yahoo," I screamed. We drove up and down the road twice and then changed positions. To make things more fun for Neil, I decided to swerve the car a bit and increase the speed considerably. Soon, I was travelling at forty-five miles per hour and could see the terrified look of complete Christmas joy smeared across Neil's face, which was also covered with a fresh layer of powder snow from the car. What a gas. Suddenly, I heard a crash. Looking out the window, I could see Neil and the chair somersaulting by the car. Whoop! They went headfirst right into the snowbank. *What a great stunt,* I thought.

Neil staggered up out of the snow and I quickly handed him a cold beer, "Wow, that was great." I went looking for the chair and discovered to my amazement that one of the runners had snapped off. We loaded the chair into the back of the car and went back to the garage. We then carefully propped the chair up on its runner in the corner where we found it. Just then Andrew's buddy Jock walked in with a great big smile, "Hey, what were you guys doing out there? It looked like fun."

"We were car sledding, but we are looking for a better sled."

"What about this?" said Jock.

"Great." We grabbed what looked to be a brand-new snow scoop and headed back out to the car.

The next thing I knew, Jock and Neil had those snowy Christmas smiles on as I dragged them up and down the road at breakneck speeds. I was laughing so hard I could barely see the road. After about an hour, we decided to go in and get some hot drinks. Everyone asked where we had been. It was getting pretty late when suddenly Andrew appeared with a major angry frown on his face. He came up to Neil and asked what we had been doing out there. I explained we were just towing each other on a board behind the car. Then he wanted to know and see what board. So Neil and I and Andrew headed out to the garage. Andrew stood in the door and carefully scanned the garage. "Rob, what were you using?" Then I froze. "What's that?" he said. Sure enough, a tiny puddle of water could be seen beside the runner of the chair. He stomped over to the chair. Neil and I quietly shared a fearful glance. Andrew then looked very closely at the puddle. He lifted the edge of the chair slowly, and to everyone's amazement, the runner fell off. "Rob, you fucking idiot, you broke my antique leather chair!"

"That's not an antique, that's a hunk of junk!" Andrew then claimed he had waited an hour at an antique auction to bid on that chair and it cost $125. "Now you owe me!" "There is no %^$$&% way I'm going to pay you a single dime for that chair!"

"You owe me cash," yelled Andrew. Then Neil spoke up, "Here, I'll pay you half, and here's my $60." Andrew's eyes lit up, but I snatched the money from Neil's hand. "Don't think of paying any money for the chair. He can fix it!"

"There is no (*& way I'm going to fix it. Give me that money!"

"No!" The screaming went back and forth as we proceeded back to the party. Jock tried to intervene but couldn't get a word in edgewise. Neil disappeared into the crowd as Andrew and I screamed at each other. "You're paying!"

"Maybe if you want cash that bad you can deduct it from the $300 I gave you for your truck door that you never fixed."

After another bout of screaming, we took a break, and I told him I was never coming back to his stinking place again. About two months later, after a bizarre incident while visiting Neil's house, I moved into his basement. The house needed a lot of work, Andrew needed some cash flow, and I needed a place to stay. At the time, it worked. In the end, it was almost five years of my life spent in the basement of the old schoolhouse in Orton.

During the few years I was holed up at my brother's, there were periods where he would go away for a week or two. The famous lists were written out on the do's and don'ts. The following is an example:

1. Numbers: fire: 855-4200
   Neighbors: Dennis Lorna Bacon (to west)
   i. Brian/Carol Thomas (goat)
   ii. Don/Sue Wright
   In Sault 705-942-9716 h
   705-946-2981 Thurs a.m.
   705-949-9461 Thurs p.m. + Fri
2. Plumbing: short showers!
   a. No more than one water appliance at a time.
   b. Make sure pump is off before leaving house—will usually run for five minutes after toilet flush. If it starts to make really weird sucking sounds and whooshing (unlikely), turn off pump. There is a switch on your right inside the door leading to the hot water tank in laundry room.
   c. Plumbers: Rory Lee Plumbing
   i. Boyes Plumbing in Erin
3. Lights: leave garage lights on (outer switch by front) if you think you'll be home late. Front overhead light is on switch by landing halfway upstairs to attic.

4. Dogs: two, three, and four cups dry in a.m. plus a can distributed equally if you have time (recycle of course!) plus 1.5 cups milk—fill up to top of milk container with hot water. Dog cookies before chaining and whenever.

5. NOT TO SLEEP ON BEDS OR COUCHES *(that is the dogs, I think!).*

6. Vet is Winegrove on Highway 24
   a. Emergency overnight kennel is Petcetera on Highway 6. (Winegrove have all medical records.)

7. Food: eat anything—chicken you cooked up is in freezer in basement.

8. Coffeepot: turn off before going to work.

9. Fan: turn on when home—green dot goes at 11:30 on dial, might need to speed it fast to get it to go around. Turn off when leaving.

10. Gun: is locked—key to unlock is on right of left drawer of desk, shells are in back of right drawer.

11. Didn't have time to get key made so if you have a chance, get one done and I'll pay you for it.

12. Furnace: must be set at -12 degrees when you leave house or go to bed; otherwise, it will run constantly and will burn up into a big cinder. Blast it to 25 when you come home and while fire is getting going.

13. Woodstove: add oak cautiously—burns really hot. Rest of wood outside is a little wet so you have to leave the holes on top open a little bit more. When I go to work, I put out in three to four pieces of wood on top of coals and leave vents about one-third of inch open. Always make sure there is water in kettle.

14. Dishwasher: put soap in both drawers. Close the one about one-half full. Put cycle to "c" with door fully closed. Don't run dishwasher or laundry if you are not in house.

Late. Gotta run. Let me know if any problems.

Oh yeah, if you want to use stove, must clean since I put some cleaner in there and forgot to take it out; therefore, the cleaner that is in there has to be removed with new cleaner otherwise you will asphyxiate your cute little self.

Years have passed, but my brother and I continue to go through bouts of angst. Whether it is bad Christmas gifts or yelling about small debt, it always seems to be something. The following is a letter he sent me a day or two before April Fool's several years ago. It is typical of the shenanigans that happens.

Ontario Ministry of Natural Resources

March 28, 2009.

Mr. Allan Gordon,
131 Meadow Park,
Sault Ste. Marie, ON
P6A 4H1

Dear Mr. Gordon:

On March 23, 2009, our Fish and Wildlife Technician, Bill Smithers, was conducting routine surveys for winter wildlife habitat near Smoke Lake, Algonquin Park, when he came across the smoldering remains of a building in the western stretches of the lake.

Upon reporting to us and upon further investigation, we have been able to trace the lease to your name (Lot 57, Peck Twp., MPAC roll number 48-03-370-002-08500-000) and are writing to inform you of this unfortunate event.

The Ontario Provincial Police, Whitney Detachment, were immediately notified and upon a brief investigation were able to detain two male individuals, who have been arrested, detained and charged under the Provincial Parks Act with trespass, intent to harm, and arson.

The burned structure appears to have been made of log, although an apparent explosion of propane tanks in the near vicinity has more or less obliterated everything except the foundation. The accused appear to have occupied the other smaller cabins on the property for some time, and have inflicted considerable damage to the interior of both.

We are writing for the benefits of your insurance company, and would be happy to meet with you to discuss building plans, should you decide to rebuild.

In the interim, please feel free to contact me should you desire further information, and accept our sincere apologies with respect to this incident.

Sincerely,

John Winnters,
Park Superintendent, Algonquin
Whitney East Gate, OMNR Complex

c. Constable Dale Martin, Whitney, OPP
Bob Smyth, ADM, OMNR, Queens Park

File: REF/ 03-876-09

April Fools - A fictitious notification created by Andrew Gordon.

Of course, the cabin didn't burn down, the letterhead was fake, and the people were fake, but all the same, it was a pretty creepy joke. I faxed it to a friend, and before I could call him, he had phoned his wife to tell her our cabin had burnt down. By the time he called his wife to say it was a joke, she had already called several people on the lake. Both my brother and I got in trouble for that. Andy Gordon lives on a farm in Damascus, Ontario, just down the road from Gordonville, with his wife Shelley and their son Ross.

Introducing Max

I never really wanted a dog. Or should I say if I ever did get a dog, I wanted a Samoyed like the one we had while I was growing up. I was very leery and suspicious when my brother Andrew came home one evening full of enthusiasm telling me that he had the perfect dog for me. He mentioned that a friend of his was splitting up with his girlfriend and that a nice dog named Max was an unwanted offspring of the relationship. So suddenly, two days later, there he was—Max.

The first week with Max wasn't too bad aside from the fact that Max wasn't really house-trained. Max's first year of life was spent in an apartment where he probably only got out once or twice all day. His first walks on the country road were funny as the rough road made him nervous to walk on it. How this would change. Now that Max was in the country, he was going to have to get used to spending most of the day outside, coming in only at night.

I should take a moment to describe Max. Max was a German shepherd / collie cross weighing about ninety pounds. He may have been a Belgium shepherd or a Belgian Tervuren. He had a foxlike tail with a fairly light thick coat with a tinge of black running down his back to his tail. The other noticeable features were his long snout and large mouth, which contained big fangs and chompers.

For the first few weeks, I was rather blasé about the idea of having a dog and was really not too keen at all about the whole idea. Andrew kept saying that we could give him back but that we should give him a chance. The first few days went by with nothing much out of the ordinary. Then, on day three, I came home from work just in time to see my brother come running out of the house with a 2×4 yelling and screaming, "I'll kill him, I'll kill him." I jumped out of the truck and ran over to see what was going on. I could see that my brother's arm had blood on it, and on closer inspection I could see a

Max a great dog.

puncture wound. "I'm going to kill that no good @!$^%*^%&@ thing—look what he did to my arm. Look at this." Andrew led me into the house, and there on the landing was a huge pile of shit. "And this!" he screamed. We went up into the main room where he pointed at his mukluks, which no longer looked like a pair of Eskimo mukluks because all the fringes had been chewed off one. Then finally with another huge scream, he said, "Look at this antique Eskimo whalebone carving." I stared at it. It looked like a normal dog bone to me. Then he screamed again and said he was going to kill that no good @$#$#& animal.

I actually had to physically restrain my brother, getting blood on my hands as I tried. I yelled, "Calm down, where is he?" Andrew led me downstairs through the water tank room under the stairs to a little known part of the house under the front of the landing. He shined the flashlight in and beat his 2×4 on the wall. Suddenly, large white teeth appeared from nowhere, snapping violently. I yelled at my brother to go outside and calm down. Andrew beat the wall one more time, screamed again, and retreated to the sound of snapping and growling. I went back under with the flashlight and discovered a very frightened dog. It took about fifteen minutes of quietly talking to get Max out of there. He seemed quite scared. I felt that when he came out of there, he trusted me, and afterward, he stuck close to me for fear of further reprisals

37

from my brother. Max and I had made some sort of bond down under the stairs. I believe it was based on trust. After that day, Max was my dog and my problem according to Andrew. Actually, with a little time, Andrew became quite fond of Max as well.

At first, Max barely seemed to know his name and the command "come" was also noted as a foreign language. Max didn't realize it, but he was about to enter the Rob Gordon School of dog training. I could tell he was smart, but he definitely needed some guidance. After about a week of screaming and yelling, I discovered that I wasn't getting anywhere. Max seemed to be heavily influenced by my brother's dog, the notorious Flashman. I tended to let Max loose when Flashman was loose, and they would hightail it out to the field behind our place to fruitlessly chase after the elusive groundhogs. Then they would disappear for hours, chasing after scents from down in the swamp. When they returned, they would usually be covered with a thick coat of mud and thousands of burrs. Time passed and Max responded best to "Bad dog," which made him stop what he was doing and look around.

The Belgium shepherd is known to be an incredibly smart dog, but was noted to find its own amusement if left alone too long. This description fit Max to a tee.

Max being playful

Max and I Go to Smoke Lake

On my first trip with Max up to my father's camp at Smoke Lake in Algonquin Park, I put Max in the back of my pickup. The pickup had a top, so I believed he would be safe back there. After about a one-hour drive, I pulled to a stoplight just outside of Alliston, Ontario, and there on the corner was a dog that looked exactly like Max. I turned to tell Max, but he was gone! That was Max chasing that little old lady! I pulled over, jumped out of the running truck, and ran down the main drag, yelling, "MAX, MAX, MAX—BAD DOG, BAD DOG—MAX, MAX—BAD DOGGG!" I grabbed him by the scruff of the neck, and although he resisted, I yanked him back to the truck, lifted him up, and rammed him in through the open window from which he had escaped. I yelled at him a couple more times "BAD DOG" before he went to sleep for a while.

Another hour down the road and poor old Max looked a little sad, so I decided to let him ride up front with me. I pulled over and walked around to the passenger side and opened the door. Max wasn't that well trained, so I didn't want him running off while I fiddled with the door. I opened the back of the truck and Max looked out questioningly. "Come on, Max, out." Max then leaped right over my right arm and dove into the muddy ditch, rolled once, and ran and jumped in the front of the truck. "MAX, BAD DOG, GET OUT!" And then he then jumped out the driver window and ran and jumped in the back. I was totally upset, and my clothes were quickly covered with mud that was everywhere in the front seat. I didn't have anything to wipe the mud-covered seat except my jacket. The rest of the trip, Max stayed in the back with the window closed, and generally, the trip was uneventful until we arrived at the dock. At that point, I let Max out of the back and he ran right over to a small white poodle. Before I could yell, "Bad dog!" the poodle went flying off the dock and plunged into the water. "She can't swim! She can't swim!" was all I could hear. I looked over and a large fat lady was screaming, "Help! Help!" I ran over and had to lie down on the dock to reach over toward the dog. I managed to grab this thing by the scruff of the neck. Max was still right there and very interested. I yelled "BAD DOG, BAD DOG," and went and tied Max to the boat.

On arrival at the camp, several people were already there. Everyone seemed glad to see my new friend Max. Max was happy to be reunited with Flashman, and they quickly made themselves scarce.

The following day after some sailing, we got the fire going, and my neighbor Sue and I got some large hot Italian sausages going on the fire, twelve in all. After watching them for about fifteen minutes, we flipped them and I decided to go for a swim. When I got out, I went over to the fire to warm up and noticed both Sue and the sausages were missing. "Sue, are we eating now?"

"We are just about to, I'm coming down with a couple of plates to get the sausages!" she yelled.

"Don't you have them?" I spoke, with some alarm.

"No," she replied. I stared at the grill of the fire and saw the flames dancing up through the grill a couple of inches. Then, glancing around, I noticed Max lying down about twenty feet away. He looked at me and burped. "MAX, BAD DOG!" I went over to him. He seemed quite content, except he no longer had any whiskers.

The rest of the weekend went off similarly with plenty of laughs. As it turned out, my new command for Max was becoming effective. "Bad dog" was a catchall phrase that seemed to work. Although his actions and intents were mostly of the curious or mischievous nature, the command always made him turn his head just as he was contemplating some new adventure.

Night of the Dead Part 1

So now I was in control of Max, or so I thought. My brother had inherited Keisha, another by-product, from a friend who had gone through a divorce. The dog was a black and gray furry ball that looked a bit like a husky. It was frisky and fast. Keisha and Max had a very strange relationship. When let off the chain, Keisha would torment Max until a chase began. What a chase it would be. They would run around and around the house and into the field and around the garage. Then, it would start all over again. After the second loop, I noticed that the game was over. Max had a determined look on his face, his ears would hook in, and the pursuit was relentless. Keisha would realize this and would soon have a look of panic on her face. Round and round. Slowly, ever so slowly, Max would gain ground. Until with a ferocious pounce and yelp, I would call out "Bad dog!" and save Keisha's life. They both would stop. This happened once a week.

Max pursues Keisha, somewhere in Orton, Ontario.

41

I recall the stress I went through in Ethiopia when news via the town fax relayed the message that Max and Keisha had run away from home. I was distraught for ten days. When I finally was able to get through on the phone to the house sitter, she said that the dogs had been found in George Town together, nearly thirty miles away! This would have been enough for Sheila Burnford, mother in law of an old friend, Lou Covello, to write another "Incredible Journey" story.

When I finally returned home nearly six months later, my brother had moved to Sault Ste. Marie for a year, and I came home to some dogs that were no longer quite mine. The dogs seemed a bit restless and a bit distracted. I remember the first night back I took them out for the walk down the country road as I had done so many times before. As I walked down the road under a warm August night, I recalled a warning my brother had given me "Be careful, those varmits will run into the cornfield and if they find their way to old farmer Brown's farm he'll kill them! He once nearly chopped the tail off of my old dog with a shovel." But that was long ago, now "Bad dog" worked for everything, or so I thought. At the turning point five hundred yards down the road, the dogs had perked up and had started to walk wildly back and forth across the road sniffing the air. *Oh no,* I thought as we walked slowly back to the house. There was a scent in the air of a strange animal. Perhaps it was the smell of a wolf or coyote. *This won't be good,* I thought. "Come on, let's go!" I yelled. But as we were near the cornfield on the left, they bolted. I yelled, "BAD DOG, BAD DOG." I continued to yell, "BAD DOG, BAD DOG." Finally, Max returned, but Keisha was gone.

I went home a desperate man and remember yelling out over the cornfield, "FUCK YOU, you stupid shit!" I went in, came out thirty minutes later, and yelled again. There was silence and nothing. "OK," I said. Andrew had warned me about the farmer down the road who had taken a shovel to his last dog and had chopped the tail off a great big Bouvier. This was not good, but it was dark and scary out, so I yelled good night and went to bed.

In the morning, I was awoken by an early morning phone call. Who could that be? I answered and what I heard was unbelievable. "Is Andy Gordon there?" The lady screaming at me sounded like a witch. "No, sorry he's not, may I take a message?"

"Yes, you can! You can tell him to come and get his damn dog! That dog is loose in our barn and has spent the night killing cats and things! That shit dog has killed twenty-three cats and my husband is going to kill that damn dog! That's what you can tell him! Tell him to come and get that crazed thing now!"

"Ah . . . right away," I replied. I hung up and ran to the front door. Fortunately, renovations were under way, so I quickly found a 2×4 about three feet long. I was going to kill that crazy thing! I ran outside, and to my complete disbelief, a completely soaked giant red rat came running at me. I took a swing and missed, then screaming, grabbed it by the neck. It was soaked right through in blood. I took it over to the hose and just soaked it completely down till there was no more blood. I then chained it to the house and screamed at it. "Screw you!" Later, I gave it some food, and within two days, I was walking it down the road again. I would use the command "Bad dog" the whole way.

The whole experience was very traumatic for me, and to make matters worse, I was frightened to leave the dogs tied up outside, lest the chainsaw massacre farmer freak from down the way would come over and chop up my buddies. My paranoia lasted quite some time.

On Finding a Fancy Watch

Rent was cheap at my brother's house, but chores were many. Cutting the grass was just one of many things I was responsible for. He had 2.3 acres, and his lawn was large with many trees. It usually took about three hours.

One lazy Saturday afternoon out in the country, I was cutting the lawn. Well, that was the day the long black Cadillac pulled up. Hell, that guy looked mean as he got out of the car. He put on a large Stetson cowboy hat and lumbered toward me. I remember him as a tall man with a large hat; he had a head of height over me. Then he spoke. "Young man," he said, "young man, I was wondering if you could help the community." Right then, I decided I needed further education; I needed more learning on motivation. "I am the caretaker of the Mimosa county graveyard and I am going away for two weeks." He continued, "I saw you with your lawnmower in the relative proximity of the graveyard and wondered if you would like to cut the grass up there. I will give you $50 a cut."

This was my lucky day, I thought. Man, did I need some extra cash.

"Well," he said, "the most important thing to remember is that the people come on Saturday, so the place has to look nice on Saturday. Some people come on Friday too, but Friday night is a good time to do the lawn. Thanks," he said again, got in the big black Cadillac, and drove off over the hill and past the graveyard.

That Thursday night, I thought that Friday morning would be the time to cut the grass because I wanted to head into Toronto for Friday night. So Friday, I was up early to get at the task right away. Unfortunately, at 6:30 a.m., the grass was deep and soaking from the dew and simply couldn't be cut. "Drats, drats, and double drats," I cursed, much like Dick Dastardly would. I would have to come back for Friday evening. I thought I saw Max snickering just like Muttley.

Muttley, Dick Dastardly's Dog

44

So Friday evening it was. And what a chore. By 9:30, I was done, I had built up a sweat, but no pretty girls were hanging on the fences nearby. I went back to the old lonely school house and a couple of dogs. Maybe my neighbor friend Don might want to come over to practice some of the tunes we were working on for the band.

The next day, I saw the cars coming and going. I realized I had an important job.

A week went by and a hot spell had come over us. The morning dew was light so this time, Friday was going to work. I was up early and decided to take Max with me. I brought the old baseball for playing catch later. I was in a bit of a hurry and did not alter my course for ground-mounted stones that had erupted at various angles from the ground over the years. The lawnmower made a grinding sound as large lumps of dolomite or limestone came flying loose in all directions, with sparks a flying. I was careful to avoid any specific names and dates. I knew my brother would wonder how the mower had gotten so dull.

Max patiently waited until I was finished, but as soon as the mower stopped, he came running over with the ball. I pushed the mower to the edge of the graveyard and admired my work. It was a beautiful summer day. I grabbed the ball from Max and ran trying to hide from him. I would make him sit and then I would take the ball to the other side of the graveyard and hide. Then I would call out. I then started trying to run around the stones. It was terrifying with him coming at me barking and seeing his bent eartips and those big teeth as he came in for the kill. I was afraid of being caught. Max had worked himself up into frenzy, and the first few seconds after he caught me might be painful. Now I threw the ball, and off, he went. He came back shortly and made me try and take the ball from him until I asked him to "drop the ball." He did and I threw it again and again. He was tireless and was having lots of fun.

Then, one time, he did not come back. Instead, I heard an urgent bark. I was startled and ran across the graveyard to see what was wrong. There Max was at the bottom of a gloriously big granite gravestone, which was slightly tilted. He was barking loudly and vigorously. "Max, what's up?" I saw the problem. There at the bottom of the gravestone was a small mound and a large hole that went down beside the gravestone. It was a gopher hole about the size of a cantalope. I called Max to come back, but then realized that the ball had probably gone down the hole. I walked up and looked down. It looked scary down there. I thought that if I put my arm down there, the vicious groundhog beast might chew it off. But Max kept barking. I said, "OK, Max, sit and no barking." I rolled up my sleeve and lay on the ground. I took one final look down the hole, but could not see anything. I reached my arm down. My hand opened trying to feel for the ball. I was surprised.

It was the strangest gopher hole because down about two feet suddenly the dirt stopped and my hand seemed to be in the corner of a wooden box. I felt around a bit, and much to my surprise, I felt a cool, sleek, small object. I pulled my arm out, and wow, I found this watch! (At this point in the story, I would have secretly undone my watch and pulled it up dangling to show any unsuspecting audience members much to their astonishment)

To complete this very odd tale, there was one more story to be told about the graveyard. On the very next Monday, I awoke and ate breakfast and hurried out the door on my way to work. I glanced to my right, and there to my surprise was the oddest sight I had ever seen. Despite the fact that the sun was not up yet, somehow a lone gravestone was completely illuminated by the sun. It looked like a ghostly portal. I quickly ran back into the house and grabbed my camera. I ran to the place where I had seen this peculiar sight and snapped a photo. I ran back inside and remembered saying to myself that no one would believe this. I really hoped the photo had worked. (Back in the days of film cameras, you never knew.) Later that night, I went back to the graveyard, and sure enough, it was the exact same grave where I had found the watch. I read the date on the stone, and it read August 17, 1845, exactly one hundred and fifty years ago to the day!

Mimosa County Graveyard before the sun was up. August 17, 1995.Orton, Ontario.

Night of the Dead Part 2

Another workday had ended. While driving back from my workplace in Mississauga, the 7:30 p.m. news on the radio said that at 8:00 p.m. sharp, the space shuttle was going to fly over just north of Toronto. I sped up. I pulled in the driveway at 7:59 p.m. The house was dark, but the sky was clear. I got out of the car and looked up. There it was, a bright steadily moving object high in the sky. Well, that was the most eventful happening all day. Routinely, I walked to the back of the house to let the dogs off their leashes. With the dogs now running around, I sat on the bench by the fire pit and could feel and breathe in the warm country air. Startled, I jumped up. Before me on the ground was a murdered groundhog! It had been cleanly chopped completely in half. Half was missing, and the remaining half was at least one and one half feet long.

My thoughts went to the crazy farmer who lived down the road. One time, he had chopped the tail off one of my brother's previous dogs when it got loose in the pigs and had sworn he would kill these dogs if they ever came in his barn again. Keisha, the keeshond, had busted into his barn about two months earlier and had terrorized the chickens and managed to wipe out the entire flock of twenty-three barn cats! So I knew this must be related; it must be some kind of warning. I called out to my brother, but after several calls, I realized he wasn't around. Finding a spade in the garage, I dug a small pit and flung the carcass in. Returning to the house, I rummaged through the empty fridge for a cold beer and walked outside in time to see the sunset over the graveyard across the field. The night became still and cool. Walking the dogs down the road, I was ever cautious of strange sounds as I waded into the mist at the bottom of the hill. The dampness sent a chill down my spine that prompted me to quicken my pace. A lone car drove slowly past the house as I returned and shut the door. I felt fairly safe with the dogs. I checked to make sure I knew where the lock was for the shotgun.

The night was peaceful and my sleep was deep. Max was at the end of my bed. It must have been 4:00 a.m. when I was eased from my sleep with a strange noise. It was a deep guttural sound. "A-WOO-GA." It repeated and became louder until I sat bolt upright. The moonlight shining in the window cast a gray light through the usually dark room and allowed me to just make out objects in the room. The sound became louder and was becoming rapid. A-WOO-GA, A-WOO-GA. What could it be? I rubbed my eyes. It was Max. He was bent like a cat with his back up. He was choking! He must have been poisoned! I jumped up, calling, "Max!" I ran up the stairs, encouraging the poor dog to follow me. The sound got louder and louder. I flung the door open and Max hobbled out. Three more A-WOO-GA's and whooshes. Up came half a groundhog, ears and all!

University Days

Phase 1 of some higher education was completed at Queen's University. I was to pursue a degree in geophysics. This decision came in a little bit of a round about way. I had once been cutting the lawn with an electric lawnmower, and when the lawnmower stopped and started to smoke badly, my first thought was that if I were an engineer, I could probably fix it. I then applied to Queen's, McMaster, and Waterloo. I was accepted at all three, but I chose Queen's because they offered residence, while the other schools said their residences were full. A week before school, a letter arrived informing me that residence was full; it apologized for the circumstances and supplied some numbers of alternate places to find accommodations. I ended up finding a place in Science 44 CO-OP. It was a kind of communal living in older houses scattered in various parts of the student ghetto surrounding the university. It was stressful as the acceptance into the CO-OP accommodations came only two days before I left for Kingston.

Rob and Greg Saunders, September, about to head to Queen's University at Kingston. 131 Meadow Park Sault Ste. Marie, Ontario

Greg Saunders and I headed down to Queen's together in his small red Datsun pickup in September.

I remember Greg dropping me off at this strange old house, 13 Sydenham, located just two blocks from the campus. Greg was going to live at West Campus for his first year. When we walked in, there were already two fellows from Ottawa in the house. They were huddled in the kitchen smoking dope. They seemed like a couple of freaks to me, but it was obvious that we were going to have to get to know them. I quickly got accustomed to the freedom of being away from home and opened a beer. The Ottawa boys joined in. Greg, who had been wearing a "Soo Y Dolphins" coat has his name changed to SYD by Scott, one of the Ottawa boys. This name has lasted to today. Not only did we have a few beers together, but also we became fast companions for our school days ahead and beyond. Our house, which held ten, was filled with future doctors, lawyers, physicists, mining and electrical engineers, nurses, and artists.

Orientation for engineers at Queen's was one week in length at the time. On our first day, we were given our tams, kilts, sporran, and dog tags, then marched through a hall and dyed purple from head to toe (a color that lasted for weeks behind the ears and under the nails). Having been in a rowdy mood, I was doing a lot of yelling, mostly toward the second year students who were beating us with large plastic bats, pouring beer on us, and generally being abusive. On our second day, we were divided into twenty groups of twenty, each group labeled 1 to 19, plus a special group for particularly bad frosh. I was in a daze from all the activity when they spray-painted my shirt and my bare arm with black, using a stencil.

"Animal"

"Oh no! What does that mean?" We were then herded into a group. I glanced around and started to feel that I actually fit into this select crowd. We were all proud, and there was Pete, one of the boys from Ottawa. We all started yelling, "Animal! Animal! Animal!" As animals, Pete and I figured our morning task was to consume at least two beers before we arrived for morning review in front of the engineering pub, Clark Hall. Various activities for all frosh groups included cleaning the shore of Lake Ontario, the golf course, peanut drives, thunder mug races and, of course, drinking. Our leaders made sure the "animals" were properly supplied.

Nightlife was more than exciting, with tales of sex, scandal, and bawdry happening to someone every night. By the time the week was over, we had painted the girl's residence and an upper year crest, Scott (our other housemate) had been thrown in jail for dislodging a parking meter, and the neighbors had had enough. The end of the week was fast approaching. Friday was retribution night, or Frosh Court, and Saturday was the infamous grease pole.

On the Friday night, a bunch of us in the "Animal" squad, after drinking several "Purple Jesus," decided to streak through the frosh court. We were supposed to be made examples of at the court. Eight of us hid in the bushes

Animal Squad Sept. 1980, Queen's University at Kingston. Me,
second from left, Pete Cottreau third from right inspecting a
fellow, who may have ended up in the wrong group.

outside the hall, peeled off our clothes, and burst into the hall, down the
stairs, and around the corner into the room. Hundreds of frosh were sitting
facing the stage where a few had been singled out to pass the cherry and were
being beaten with bats and having beer poured on them. When we rushed
in screaming, the crowd went wild. As we crossed the stage and descended
the steps to the side entrance, about ten second year students had jumped
in among us to prevent us from leaving. Suddenly, I found myself caught
between two "Frecs" (second year engineering frosh group leaders). Two
friends were also trapped. As we sped away, I realized that I had never before
leveled anyone with one punch like I managed to do then. Running back
across the beer-soaked stage, I slipped and slid about ten feet. Before I knew
it, I was out of the main stage door and falling on the steps.

Finally outside, I discovered I had cut my knee. Warm blood was running
down my knee. I ran out into the street, only to cross in front of a police car.
I ran and ran and hid in the dark. It took about two hours to get back to my
clothes. Everyone met back at my place to discuss the events, drink some beer,
and prepare us for the grease pit in the morning.

The Grease Pit

Queen's engineering had a reputation for robust frosh week activities. Following the week of degradation at the hands of upper year students, the principle highlight of all activities during frosh week was the dreaded climbing of the grease pole. A tam that is nailed to the top must be retrieved before the engineering year is officially recognized. There were great rumors floating around as to how bad it would be. On that sunny fall morning, we were being herded into large U-haul trucks until we could barely fit. There was no time to think. It was more than a bit frightening. After a very long drive to a secret location in the country, the truck stopped and backed up. Suddenly, the door was unlatched and opened. I strained to see over the crowd but quickly got a firsthand look as we hopped to the ground.

The grease pit was large and was steaming with mist and smoke. The second year students were chanting and walking around with dead horse heads and various other dead roadkill animals. These were then thrown into the pit. A megaphone quickly blurted out the rules: "OK, Frosh. At the bell, jump into the pit, climb to the top of the greased steel pole, and retrieve the tam-o'-shanter that is nailed to the top. You do not become an official engineering year until the tam is off!" I quickly realized why they had warned people with any open cuts not to get in the rat-infested oily mess. It was too late for me as the sea of people started to move forward. The pole was said to be one of the goal posts removed from University of Toronto following an infamous football win years ago over the University of Toronto. The entire pole seemed to be thirty feet high. The U-haul trucks now circled the pit, and the second and third year students had what appeared to be bushels and bushels of tomatoes and water balloons. The bell rang, and amid the chaos, the pit started to fill with humans. Girls were not allowed in the pit. Much like Flashman from George McDonald Fraser's chronicles, I desperately looked for a way out of this mess. The pole was covered with thick black axle grease. The first chore was to clean the pole. I quickly started climbing because I wanted to stay out of the pit with my taped-up knee from the night before at frosh court. I made it up to the third tier and people were screaming while tomatoes were flying. My shoes with plastic soccer studs were causing a great deal of pain below. The lead man was now quite a bit above me, and cheers were loud as he neared the top. I turned and looked around. It was an impressive event for sure. Suddenly, a rock (turned out they were throwing frozen tomatoes) hit me squarely in the forehead. I started to wobble and desperately tried to grab on. With a sickly thud, I slumped down into the pile, pulling with me the entire upper tier. We careened down to the layers of humans below like bowling pins, but only with slick thuds and yelps. The tower was lost, and the lead man quickly followed with a fast fireman drop into the rest of us. Over and over, we went. Finally, the tomatoes had run out, and we made consistent progress until at fifty-one minutes, our lead man tore a significant piece of tam off and it was over. My leg became quite infected and later was amputated!

A year later, as a second year FREC (frosh group leader), I enjoyed the night before activities with my same buds and slept in a U-haul. We waited the retrieval of the pole from a secret spot for midnight setup and the creation of the pit. Apparently, the driver of the truck with the pole had made a narrow escape from some people who had tried to drive them off the road, possibly U of T students attempting to retrieve the pole. When the driver finally arrived, he came up to me and announced in front of everybody that he had seen Rob Gordon in the car that had chased them. Of course, I denied this and my friends who I was with in the cab of a parked U-haul, attested to my claims; however, my reputation as a rabble-rouser took on a new dimension and unwarranted dimension. Two years later, a few apologies came.

September 1980, Kingston, Canada. Photo from Golden Words,
Queen's Engineering newspaper, used by permission.

Where's the Vacuum Cleaner?

Alfies, the Queen's University school pub, advertised for some time that there was to be a concert the night of my birthday. My friends and I agreed to celebrate down at the pub. We all felt the big night was going to be a blast, and we were all excited. We were first in line at the pub and ran to get an optimal table: close to the bar, the girls' washroom, and halfway to the stage. Once settled in, the first two jugs disappeared quickly. Everyone was having a great time and it was only 7:45. The band was to come on at 9:00 p.m. Alas, something went totally wrong.

Over at the next table, there were four gorgeous blondes. Within a few minutes of smiling and nodding, the waiter appeared with seven shots of tequila. "It is from the girls at the next table," he winked. Wow. *This was going to be fun for everyone,* I thought. But the girls wouldn't let me distribute the drinks. "No, they are for you, we heard it was your birthday." The chants became loud, and it was all too easy keeping those girls smiling as I drank my way into their hearts. As it turned out, it was right past their hearts and into oblivion. The birthday was at its peak and it was only 8:00 p.m.

Suddenly, the table collapsed, the room become blurry, and smashing glass could be heard all around. The next thing I knew I was being thrown out the door. Bang. Scott and Pete followed. "You ass," they cried. "Why did you dive on to the girl's table?"

Suddenly, I felt completely sober; I apologized to my friends and cried, "We don't have to be there to have fun." I ran out onto the road, and wham, a car hit me. The driver and Scott and Pete came over and looked down at me. Within no time, they had me up, and Syd and I were going home. I pleaded and feigned I was sober. "Please, let's go downtown." Finally, they complied. We made it about a block and I started banging into things. "Take that," they cried and literally dragged me home, in the door, and threw me on the couch. My head went black as it hit the old heavy arm of the couch with a thud!

A little later, my eyes opened and the room began to spin, ooooooooooo. Suddenly I sat up and said "help" to myself. About two tons of food appeared on the floor between my feet. I slouched back onto the couch, gone for good. The morning came too quickly. I opened my eyes and something hit me. What's that smell? Yikes! I ran to the cupboard and grabbed the old vacuum, vvvvvruuuuuuum, and the mess was gone and my parents were knocking on the door to take us to Chez Piggy's for breakfast.

About a month later, Erlene, a large African Canadian who lived on the second floor, came pounding on my door on the third floor. "Rob, where's the vacuum?"

"Ah? Hmm? I'm not sure, maybe on the, oh, yeah, it's in the basement cupboard."

"What's it doing there?" she said in an arrogant tone.

"I don't know." A few minutes later, I could hear the hum of the vacuum in the room below me. Suddenly, there was a loud popping sound, like a giant popcorn machine going off. "BANG." Then there was a horrible bloodcurdling scream. All the members of the house came running to see what the problem was. On reaching Erlene's room, I could see that the vacuum had backed up and the lid had popped, blowing all the contents of the machine across her room in a giant stinky dustbowl. Freeze-dried food was scattered all over Erlene's room. I quickly made my way back up the stairs and back to my homework.

Ramsey the Sheep

During the year, there were a number of social events we attended for our year, but some of the more interesting ones involved going to the senior year's events. One Friday evening, my friend Paul Healy and I were attending a Science 83 party and the place was packed. I had nicknamed Paul "Toolee" after the big Indian friend of Jack Nicholson in *One Flew over the Cuckoo's Nest* because of Paul's lumbering size, dark hair, and overall mean look. Paul was a great guy with a very good sense of humor.

As the evening progressed, it became apparent there was a special event about to happen. On the stage was a stand with a sheet over it. They announced the unveiling of the second year's new mascot "Ramsey the Sheep." It looked hilarious; it was a stuffed sheep with ram's horns attached. Immediately, I was coming up with a plan to steal it. I managed to get the idea planted in Toolee's head that if I created a diversion, he could grab it and duck down the back stairs of Clark Hall. He nodded and said, "Sure, great idea." He had a "sure, sure" look on his face that I didn't pick up on. With the plan in place, I made my way to the left of the stage and, on cue, had an epileptic fit. People came running to help me and I knew our plan would work. However, as I was slowly helped up, I saw Toolee bent over, laughing his face off! He then told me that he had never thought our plan would work and hadn't planned to follow through at all. I was frustrated, and after a couple of more beers, I said bye to Toolee and headed home.

I was halfway down the stairs and heard a big commotion. Apparently, several students of the second year class did not want the beast and tried to stomp it. Several of the Science 83 executive committee rushed by me with Ramsey and placed him in the Engineering Society office, which was adjacent to the pub exit on the second floor of Clark Hall. I found myself alone in the stairwell, so I could not resist testing the door. It opened. There on the pool table was Ramsey. The room was quiet. Without a thought, I grabbed it and ran out the door and down the stairs. The bouncers saw me and yelled out in alarm. I ran and ran with yelling and hooting sounds fading far behind me as I raced across Pervert's Park. I took a special way home and crept up the back way like Batman. I told Pete and Scott about my caper, but they were not impressed. A knock came at the door and it was Toolee. He said the whole place was in an uproar, and no one knew who took it. We laughed and played around taking silly photos and throwing darts at it and then launched phase 2 of our brilliant plan.

Toolee (Paul Healy) with Ramsey, just after the heist, Kingston Ontario, fall, 1980

We would hold Ramsey for ransom. For a hiding place, I had found an old window that opened out under the front steps in the basement. The window was hidden from direct view. A week passed and a note appeared in the paper that threatened the frosh that took the sheep. The following week, we replied with a list of our demands, which was quite simple: ten cases of beer. The dialogue and rhetoric continued for a while.

Science '83 News

Last Saturday night Sci '83 had a marvelous evening during its year opening smoker. The only black mark to speak of occurred near the end of the evening. In an obvious crime of passion, a slimy gang of sexually frustrated upper year engineers sheepnapped Ramsey, our year mascot. We expect him returned quickly - and no fatter. Necrephiliac beastiality is out with us guys.

On the happier side, the official "custodian of the sheep" are Dick Workington, Bruce Farrand and James Matheson.

It's time to get your entry for our T-shirt logo contest ready. We would like it to be one colour and full size. As for content - keep our little animal in mind. Entries should be submitted to the ENGSOC office by October 1.

Get psyched everyone! We have buses going road tripping to Montreal leaving this Saturday morning, and returning the same day for the nominal charge of $8 return. This offer is even extended to non Sci '83 members!

Science 83 NEWS

Dear Fellow Yearlings,

Negotiations are still underway concerning the release of Ramsey, held captive since his abduction from the Engineering Embassy during our last smoker. In a video recording Ramsey said he misses his kid (ha, ha) and wants to come home. So let's not forget Ramsey or give in to ridiculous demands.

Other things which must not be forgotten are Science 83 paraphanalia. There are still a few Science 83 ties, T-shirts and "84 Sucks" buttons available. All these items are ideal for Frosh Week (especially the last one) and should be purchased before the end of the year. Lists for signing up to buy them will be passes around classes tomorrow. (Thems that pay first gets first.)

Once properly attired you will be ready for many social events. A few ideas for next year's social scene are a Science 83 ski trip, a movie night featuring one of film's greatest (probably the worst movie we can get, ie. something like The Killer Tomatoes), a scavenger hunt encompassing various parts of Ontario (ie. bring back a menu from the Colonade Pizzaria in Ottawa or get on CFRC and state that you love Mildred Snotgrass), a joint Science 83-82 dance and of course road trips and smokers. Any other thoughts or comments are welcome. Feel free to contact any of the newly elected executive listed in last week's G.W. P.S. See next week's G.W. concerning the repainting of our defaced crest outside Vic Hall.

$ci '83

Your dumb Mascot eats a lot and I'm getting a little tired of feeding it. If you want your Mascot back you will comply with the following demands:

For the safe return of Ramsey we demand 10 cases of beer! So as not to give ourselves away we want the following:

1 case Golden	1 case Buckeye
1 case Blue	1 case Ex
1 case Brador	1 case I.P.A.
1 case 50	1 case O.V.
1 case Extra Stock	
1 case Moosehead (brewed in New Brunswick, they import it in the States)	

The time and place of the exchange will be arranged. To prove Ramsey is O.K. this picture is enclosed:

Signed: Some silly Frosh who can relate to the Animal in Ramsey.

P.S. Funny, isn't it?, that some silly Frosh have your dumb Mascot, eh!

News from *Golden Words*, the Queen's Engineering Weekly paper, 1981. Used by permission.

One night, there was a knock at the door, and a girl's voice asked for Rob Gordon. I naturally opened the door. There in front of me charging in were commandos with camouflage suits and painted faces; they had me before I reached Scott's room. About ten people searched the house, but no Ramsey. I finally broke free and got a few to follow me to the alley where I quickly lost them. Ramsey was still in our clutches.

Unfortunately, when the school year ended, we still had Ramsey. Apparently, Ramsey was not liked by about half of the second year class and so they had voted to refuse to negotiate for Ramsey's freedom. So on the last day of school, we tied him to the roof of Greg (Syd) Saunders truck and he, Dave Ghent, and I headed home. On the way home, we stopped at a Dairy Queen in Parry Sound, and a little old lady came up to us. She was quite upset with the treatment of the poor little sheep. She thought that it would be "much too cold having to stand on the roof like that."

That summer, my father had some mysterious calls regarding a sheep. Ramsey was on a shelf in the basement while I was out in British Columbia enjoying my first summer of exploration work for Anaconda Canada.

4   Wednesday, March 4, 1981

SCI' 83
(again)

We've been waiting for a reply and we haven't heard anything yet! We have also discovered the true value of Ramsey-quite an expensive treasure isn't he. Because you have waited so long, the price has gone up. Forget the Moosehead beer and add a case of Canadian and a case of Stock ale. Plus a Hockey set-that is the coleco one in the Consumer's Catalogue with the sturdy legs-$29.00. You might have noticed in the picture last week a small thing in the rear of Ramsey. Just a dart to keep him drugged up and stoned. I suggest to you that you reply this week, or the next time you see Ramsey it will be a lamb chop at a time.

Signed the Same Silly Frosh who keeps on making '83 LOOK LIKE A BUNCH OF LOST SHEEP.

Wednesday, March 11, 1981   **9**

Science 83 NEWS

Time to warm up your frisbees and dust off the running shoes because hopefully, spring is on its way. Talking of spring reminds me of a poem,

Spring has sprung,
The grass has riz,
I wonder where our Ramsey is?

Well the frosh are giving him an extended Reading Week and its time for him to come home and get back to those who love him. To thank his hosts for their trouble, we are willing to donate them a Coleco hockey game to grace their recreation parlour and to entertain their simple minds. On top of this we will even provide a case of Buckeye, provided 84 can deliver Ramsey safe and sound. We expect to hear a reply in the near future.

On a different note, Sci 83 ties, T-shirts and 84 sucks buttons are still available. Someone will be circulating an order sheet in each section. Order now and avoid the rush later. Remember, we want to make a good impression next September.

Ferret

News from *Golden Words*, the Queen's Engineering Weekly paper, 1981
Back-and-forth dialogue was required, note they are starting to break.

When we returned for second year, we finally negotiated a deal for the release of Ramsey. We ended up getting two cases of beer and a Coleco hockey set, which was badly needed because the set we had from first year had been played out. Ramsey was returned, only to be eventually stolen by the dissident then–third year engineering students that never wanted him in the first place. He was finally burned and thrown in Lake Ontario. A year later, he floated ashore and reappeared as their new mascot. The mascot was now Blacky, the sheep.

The Nightmare on Elm Street

In second year, I found that the second year executive had decided that Rob Gordon was just too bad a dude and that most of the people making up the local engineering rag *The Golden Words* were prone to shun him. Not that I cared, but I noticed. They knew of my secret relationship to the third year mascot Ramsey and thought that was in bad taste. In addition, during the evening of the grease pole setup party, one of my own year swore that I was in a car that tried to run their truck off the road, the night (we) the second years were bringing the famed grease pole back from its hiding spot. I had my friends Dave Cameron, who later became an F18 fighter pilot, and Toolee with me to testify that I was in fact at the grease pit, waiting like the rest of the team for the pole's late night arrival. In any event, by third year, I was finally settling down a bit. Here is a simple story that tells of the only night of the year I went out by myself and did not happen to have one single beer.

One evening after study, I went to Clark Hall to the year's election review. Marci Morris, a very nice, social girl who was closely associated with the group that did not give me the time of day, not only noticed me, but asked me if I would be interested in coming by after the "tea pub" for cookies and more tea! I decided to go to prove in part that as an apple, I was not rotten to the core. Yes, I stole the mascot of an upper year, but no, I did not try to steal the grease pole from my very own year despite an eyewitness (asshole) who claimed I did. Marci was a girl with a big smile and would always make a point of talking with me despite my reputation as a rogue in the eyes of several members of our class. She was surprised I hadn't had anything to drink and that I demonstrated true sincerity in walking her home safely. When we got to her place, she asked me in for tea and popcorn. Unusual, I thought, but what the heck, I might as well show off my hidden nice side, so I accepted. We went into the bright yellow kitchen and she introduced me to her friends.

One of the girls was named Tracy. After the popcorn was half finished, the phone rang, Tracy picked it up and quickly said, "I am sorry, but I don't want to talk to you. No, I don't want to talk to you, sorry, good-bye." She hung up and started to cry and went upstairs. I continued to eat the popcorn. After a few minutes of quiet, they briefly told me about her boyfriend who didn't want the relationship to be over. The phone rang again; this time they asked me to answer the phone. After the fellow asked for Tracy, I told him my name was Toolee, and if he called again and bothered the girls, I would have to pound him. I hung up. The phone immediately rang again; this time we just picked up and hung up.

After fifteen minutes, I had finally just finished off the popcorn. I realized Marci and I were not meant for each other in a romantic way, so I was considering how to politely leave. Then the doorbell rang. Tracy, who had come downstairs and was hanging in the kitchen, went to answer the door. Suddenly, Tracy went running upstairs bawling; Marci went out to the door and came back in a terror. The girls were in a panic. Marci came back into the kitchen and said to me, "He's here!"

"Who?" I asked.

"It's Tracy's old boyfriend." She asked me to go and tell him to leave. I cautiously walked around the corner, and there was a clean-cut commerce student sitting in the living room. He made no sound. Then the fellow got up and stood at the bottom of the stairs calling, "Tracy, Tracy, come downstairs." Then he went back into the living room. I stood up and walked around the corner into the living room and asked the guy if he would leave. I mentioned that this was inappropriate, and if he wasn't invited in, he was trespassing and we would call the police. He then went and sat down in a big chair on the other side of the room. I went to the kitchen and called the operator, "Get me the police." I mentioned the events to the police and was asked where he was now; I said, "I'd be right back." Walking into the living room again, I noticed he had been at the bottom of the stairs; the girls upstairs were in hysterics, and Marci went to see how Tracy was.

I was getting a bit agitated when he started calling out for Tracy again. "Tracy, Tracy!" he yelled like Marlon Brando calling for Stella. The next few moments were tense as I mentioned that he was going to be in a lot of trouble and he should just leave. I ran back to the phone and mentioned he was not prepared to leave and they should come quick. I looked around the kitchen and wondered if there was any beer in the fridge. Then I went back out to the living room.

I walked over to the chair and said, "Listen, pal, you are going to be in so much shit if you don't leave." He just kept calling for Tracy. I took two steps toward him as I was now thinking of just grabbing him by the scruff of the neck and throwing him out. One more step and he jumped up with a rather large knife in his hand.

At this point, I put my hands up in the air and said, "Whoa, easy, if you want to stay, hey, that's fine by me." I backed up and started to wish I was the evil Gordo again and not a late-night teatotaller trying to change my image. I took two steps back as he approached with the knife, he was still calling, "Tracy, come down." I was scared and my heart was pounding. At some point, the room got very small, my mind raced, and suddenly, I made an irrational decision. My mind flashed to a comment Toolee had made to me once in another circumstance, "Are you going to let that guy do that to you?" *No was my answer,* I thought, and action had to follow. Instantly, I leapt at the guy and, much like a Hawaii-Five-O scene, grabbed his right wrist with my left hand. Then, there was a big commotion. Chairs and coffee tables went flying. I became rather numb as the struggle went back and forth. All the while, my mind was saying, "You better win, Rob." Then, exactly like I had seen in all those movies, I smashed his hand against the wall until the knife dropped. I then kicked it into the hall cupboard that was open. But when I took my eyes off him to watch the knife slide away, he kneed me in the groin. At this point, things got ugly. Just like the old radio skit, *The Champ,* I lost it! I grabbed him by the scruff, lifted him, and dropped him to the floor. I then jumped on him with one knee and was about to haul off and smash his face, when the front door burst open and another assailant yelled, "Hey! Break it up, Gordo," and jumped me, knocking our knife boy free. The new fellow in the room thought that I was the troublemaker. Fortunately, for me and the newcomer, the girls now were yelling that I was the good guy and we managed to re-apprehend the bad guy. I managed to boot him a good kick in the ass as he headed out the door to wait for the police who had been called.

"Oh, Gordo, you saved us" was now the banter. I was pumped and felt like a champ, but I still wanted to pummel the guy. He was now sitting on the steps outside with his head down, being held by the other guy. I wanted more popcorn, and I needed a beer. With only minutes until the police arrived, I went outside and mercilessly picked him up and threw him over the steps; he landed on his head and was in discomfort when the police arrived. After a few hours at the police shop, I finally staggered home. It was about to get light out. I knocked on my buddy Scott's door and said, "You won't believe what happened to me tonight." Without any thought and having just been woken up at 4:30 a.m. in the morning, Scott set up a tape recorder and recorded the whole story, fresh. The tape exists, my transcription here has a few less expletives.

Within a few days, I had received a hero card from the girls and an apology card from the criminal. The criminal had turned out to be a very prominent commerce student. Although the ending was happy for most of us, we all would have been happy if it had never happened. However, I did manage to get a "hero" badge in the process.

Tues. Nov. 24, 1981

Dear Rob,

I don't expect you will forget me, but I hope perhaps you will forgive me for my actions of Sunday morning last. All I can say is that I am very sorry and ashamed, and hope that somehow this helps.

Sincerely,

A card from the assailant.

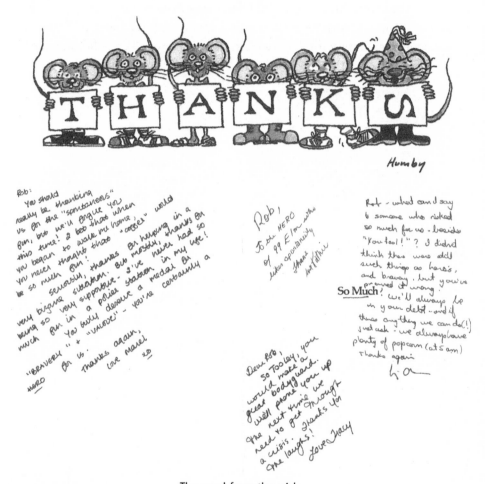

The card from the girls.

It really happened, all these stories are true!

Homecoming, a Parade Story

While sitting in the Clarke Hall pub one Friday afternoon, my friends and I decided that we should enter a float in the Homecoming Parade that was planned for the following day. In those days, we really thought we could do anything. So we actually thought we could pull something off with just five bucks from everyone. With sixty-five dollars though, I was unsure what we might end up with. In a worst-case scenario, it would mean more beer for Saturday. After a few calls around town, we finally struck gold. The fellow at the wrecking yard had just the car for us, and it was only going to be $65 bucks.

Three of us went north of town via cab to the wrecking yard and presto, a '62 Valiant. What a beauty. In the end, it was a sad story because this was simply a perfect, beautiful car. The yardman took me for a spin. He managed to get it up to forty miles per hour down the track between the piles of junk. I was terrified. Wow, the car was way too good for us. But we took it anyway. We arranged that he would drop it off at Dave Cameron's house later that evening, and he would pick it up from the stadium after the weekend. He stipulated that he really wanted the battery back, but did not care about the car. Wow, arguably the best $65 ever spent.

That night we met at 10:00 p.m. to wreck the car and get it ready for the parade. People brought axes and a lot of beer and we hacked and beat the old car to pieces. The plan was to meet first thing in the morning and get ready for the parade at noon. Wow, did we have fun. After hours of violent demolition, there was still a big problem. When we started it, it still hummed like a bird.

The $65 car, finally ready for the parade.

This would not do, so we tilted it up and chopped the muffler off with the axe. Now it was starting to sound good. We were all painted like Indians and were itching to barge into the parade that would start down the street in three hours. We got ready and took a group picture just before the parade started.

The unofficial Science 84 parade entry: (left to right) Ringer, Paul Healy, Dave Ghent, Ed Koopman, Peter Cottreau, Rob Gordon, Scott Bulbrook, John Ryan, Peter Everett. (front):John Lewis, Chris Moon (driving), Dave Cameron, Mark Byron, John Paul.

By noon, we were hyped and had very good school spirit. Then, an MGB convertible drove by with a sweater freak and a blonde. Someone, probably Dave Cameron (future F18 fighter pilot) lobbed a big water balloon onto the chick in the car. Following some initial cursing and then another barrage of water balloons, the car sped off. Then we rolled the car back and all fourteen of us piled on. Wow. Suddenly, the sirens were blazing, and we were totally surrounded. We all ran like jack-in-the-boxes. When I realized it wasn't me that the police had in the back of the cruiser, I darted off to fetch my camera for a quick picture.

En route to the parade, we were busted.

The police went nuts. The good cop / bad cop scenario was just ugly as some of us (Flashman technique) watched from the bushes. Our only sober person, Chris Moon, was having the book thrown at him because of the various infractions the car posed. These included flat tires, no wipers, no indicators, no muffler, no lights, no seatbelts, open beer in the vehicle, no brake lights, etc. After about forty-five minutes, they finally agreed that it was a float, but we would only be allowed on the street if we pushed it. This was good news for us. Fortunately, the police did not have an official list of parade participants. The parade had now started, so we anxiously started pushing our float down the street followed closely by the police. As we got close, we asked Chris Moon to start it up as we needed to barge into the parade. Chris was reluctant, but under some intense peer pressure, he turned the key. Fa fa rroom fa room, and there we were. We started our barrage of big ketchup-coated tampons on any unsuspecting person nearby, including other floats and spectators. Wow, what a reaction. We cut in and out and caused as much humanly fun chaos as possible. The ride lasted about twenty-five minutes, and it was great.

Golden Words coverage of the parade.

Once we got to the game, we gave her the heave-ho and flipped it. We were never to see it again. Upon reflection, it was probably a crime scene that we helped destroy.

Guess What a Dieffenbachia Plant Tastes Like?

Fortunately, participating in homecoming parades did not happen every year. But back in 1984, I realized I needed to have a costume for the parade that could be remembered. I searched the house high and low for something to wear that would look special. In the basement, I found what looked to be the ideal costume. It might need a bit of work, but that was fine.

Ross Farrar, the son of the head of the geology department and one of my oddball friends, had passed through town several months earlier. At that time, he was quite proud of what he had captured on one of his adventures. His problem was that he needed a place to store it and convinced me to put it in the basement. What he had found in Toronto was to be part of my costume. It was sad that it had been sitting by the furnace, collecting greasy dust. I carried it upstairs and looked at it, pondering my situation. What Ross had found was a giant plastic Christmas bell. This bell was the kind of bell found dangling from streetlights on cold crisp winter nights in small towns and cities across Ontario. Where he got this bell, no one knows. But there it was in a sack in our basement.

So on the following Saturday morning, I decided that the time had come for the world to be introduced to a new superhero. His name would be: the Human Bell. It didn't take long to shape the costume. I cut the bell into three pieces: top, middle, and bottom. The bottom part of the bell was fashioned to look like a miniskirt that should scare anyone. I put it over my head and pushed it down until it was tight around my hips. It fit perfectly.

The middle portion of the bell was cut and placed around my midsection, and the top portion of the bell was fashioned to be a perfect fitting hat. It was as if the bell had been manufactured to fit perfectly for me something like a ShaZaam suit. The beautiful Saturday morning was helped along by several bottles of beer from a case that had been brought over by some comrades,

71

shortly after the beer store opened at 10:00 a.m. As preparations continued for the parade, I noticed more and more people were stopping by, and the kitchen was full of people; most of them were wondering what I was up to. The air in the apartment contained wisps of smoke from strange people wandering through.

I was almost ready to go, and there on the counter was the last thing I needed to complete my costume. It was a plant that sort of looked like a fern or some celery. I removed my hat and proceeded to cut a hole in the top of the bell that would be wide enough to put the plant through. I grabbed the plant and walked to the kitchen to find a bag for it. My roommate, Ian Shenkel, was up in arms. He started to rant that I was destroying another one of his precious things. I assured him that it was not my intention. I continued to rip the plant out of the bucket and placed it in a plastic bag. With my roommate yelling in the background, I tied the bag off with some elastic. Now, with the plant and some dirt in the bag, I said, "There, you see, nothing is going to happen to your nice little plant." Ian was in hysterics as usual, "I got that dieffenbachia from home and my mother wants it back," he screamed. "Yeah, yeah, nothing is going to happen to your plant." I fitted the leaves up through the hole in the bell that was to be my hat and carefully placed the bag on my head as I placed my unusual hat on my head. One check in the mirror revealed that I definitely was dressed to kill, and there was a good chance I would win a giant prize for this costume. Mingling in the kitchen for about twenty minutes and a few beers later found me out on the street on a bright sunny day heading to the football game. "Hey, look at that, a human bell," someone yelled.

Well, off to the game we trundled. By the time we hit the game, the crowd was swaying and the people I was with were swaying and I was swaying. It was a great day, early fall, sunny and warm, and fun. In the background, a football game raged.

By the second half, the game was a bit of a blur. Then a stranger walked up to me. He pointed to my head and said, "What kind of plant is that?" I was flabbergasted. How rude to interrupt my random wanderings with a serious question. "It's celery!" I said dismissively. Then, as I was about to leave he said, "That is not celery!" I said, "Listen chump, this is celery." This conversation took place in front of the front-row seating. The entire bleachers on the east side of the field in front of us were packed. I reached up and broke off a stock. Before I knew what the heck I was doing, I bit the stock and chewed it well for about five chews. "There, see! Celery!" Suddenly, I realized something was terribly wrong.

The human bell costume just before the addition of the dieffenbachia.

My tongue grew three sizes that day, just like the Grinch's heart, in three dimensions, and all this at a very rapid rate. It felt like someone had put a very big pincushion in my mouth, and it was harshly pricking everywhere, including down my throat. My eyes started to bulge and I couldn't breathe. All I could think of was that I needed some liquid in my mouth immediately. I grabbed at the first person I saw and tried to get their drink; they pushed me away, and I grabbed at another and another. I was in a frenzy. It was like the old horror movie of the man with the iron mask at the party where it just keeps getting tighter and tighter as he runs from guest to guest. My antics had caught the attention of the whole crowd now, with loud stampng, yelling, and chants of "HUMAN BELL, HUMAN BELL!" I finally grabbed a wineskin from some fellow, and despite his yelling to give it back, I chugged the wine into my throat. The beverage was tilted up and was pouring down my throat and all over my face. "HUMAN BELL, HUMAN BELL!" I could feel the swelling subside, but it was too late. The crowd wanted more. "HUMAN BELL, HUMAN BELL!" I finally got the heck out of there. I ripped the stupid plant out of my skullcap and threw it over a fence on the way home.

When I finally staggered in the house at about 11:30 p.m., I was reduced to a partial bell, teetering but not ringing. I was immediately assaulted by screaming. "Rob, where is my plant?!?"

The Very Last Day of School, or Henry Gets Arrested

The afternoon ended after three hours of complete stress and anxiety. I had just finished the last exam of my arduous university career. *Man, why me?* I thought to myself. Am I absolutely out of it? I thought that despite all my effort, I would surely have to repeat this exam. This is a topic that must be beyond most people. Imaginary waves of something hit a boundary and need to be explained by boundary equations. Fields of energy spinning through the air all explained by famous Maxwell and his equations. Yikes!

Why did I pick geophysics again? Thanks, Dad. I still remember, he said choose something that contributes to our global society. I thought plate tectonics was global, so here I was in the fourth year electromagnetic exam. It was over, and I stood up. *That was a bad experience,* I thought to myself. Little did I know that this experience was going to contribute to a life of recurring dreams about not having studied enough for a final exam. I slowly walked to the back of the room and came upon a central group of my classmates (we were only eleven in the geophysics option), and there seemed to be a disturbance. To me, it was face the facts, it was clear; I must not have been paying attention. To the rest, it was political outrage. "They are not allowed to do that!" they collectively yelled.

"We did not take that and I never knew they were going to include that!" The crowd grew to about eight people, yammering away outside, the exam hall in Dunning, the civil engineering building. *Well,* I thought to myself, *this was not as bad as the time I fell asleep in the surveying exam in first year and had to do the whole exam in forty minutes.* And I passed that. What's the problem? I yearned to be a part of the conversation, but the crowd was getting louder, and suddenly, they decided to march to the prof's office and rebel. Well, I will follow, just to see what happens.

They were up in arms. We all stomped over with me cautiously behind.

The girls in the class started the protest and the guys, who were trying to impress the girls the most, joined in and basically lambasted the professor for lambasting us on the exam. Suddenly, I heard words of consolation and words of joy. The professor stood up and holding his arms up and open like a Sunday service, said, "Listen, none of you have to worry. You will all do fine, I am sure!" At that point, I barged to the front of the crowd to make sure he saw me. I bent my knees so as not to appear like a goon and put on a sad face like the rest. Eye contact was made, and I knew I did it. After all that time, I was going to get a degree in geophysics. I slipped to the back and started to get tall. I was happy and we needed to party. "Hey, come to my house and let's celebrate."

"Yeah!" everyone said and off we marched. We were all so happy. Nothing could stop us now. This was great.

A few were going to get the beer, some were going to change, and some were going to eat. We met after the second period of a Montreal game. We all watched the game and then after guzzling a bunch of beer decided to go downtown to the Irish pub to have a good party. There was Marlene, Paula, and Barb, Henry, Peter, Andy, and myself. We walked out the door and around the back. At that point, I said, "Hey, why don't we climb that ladder and get on the roof, we can walk all the way downtown on the rooftops." These were the rooftops of the buildings that lined Pricecess Street, the main drag in Kingston Ontario.

Well, it seemed like a good idea at the time. After five buildings, we came to our first problem. We were going to have to leap about twelve to fourteen feet to get to the next roof. I assured everyone it was possible and took a few steps back as if to run. With screams of no, I stopped and looked down. Wow, look at that, an old carriage! Let's climb down and use that! Well, we all clambered down, and yes indeed, this idea would work. The girls could get in the carriage and the guys could pull the two-wheeled contraption. Off we went, clip-clop, what a laugh. Everyone was having fun, and we rode all the way down Division Street until we were right downtown. When we got down behind the Irish bar, we realized we needed to ditch the old antique buggy. What luck, we had paused in front of an architect's office. It looked like a beautiful place to leave the giant buggy. We pulled it up on the lawn and placed one of the wheels right on top of this pile of rocks in front of the office. It looked like it was a corporate decoration. We laughed and laughed and headed to the bar. After lots of dancing and carrying on, we found ourselves together again at closing time and started to walk the long walk home.

Then someone said (quite probably me), "Hey, what about the buggy?" Instantly, everyone said, "Let's get it." Well, we took it from the architect's yard and slowly pulled it onto the street. We were facing south and figured taking the back streets would be the best idea. So we loaded up a few girls on the cart and grabbed the front and started to pull forward. Within thirty seconds of getting organized for the return trip, a police cruiser pulled around the corner and came straight down the street toward us. It slowed immediately. People were getting very nervous. I decided some leadership was necessary and I spoke up. "Listen, just put on a straight face and do exactly what I say." Then I added, "Keep going and pretend that we are meant to be doing this. Be very serious and under no circumstances look sideways and do not panic." Everyone complied. We inched forward; all of our smiles were gone. Slowly, the police car came toward us. "Heads down, guys, just pretend we are working!" At five miles per hour, the police car passed us. Relief started to crawl up my back.

Then, suddenly, without warning, the formidable brake lights of a yellow police cruiser came on! In retrospect, I am sure this is a proven technique that they use to test suspicious events. Well, it worked. Without wasting a precious second, I yelled, "RUN" at the top of my lungs. Then, just like a well-oiled army unit, everyone obeyed. We all split in all directions. I ran straight ahead and down the street. I heard a door slam and a car come down the street in full reverse. I ran around the corner and as fast as I could across the street. Down past five houses including Flora McDonald's (a retired federal politician) and then a sharp left and down an alleyway and . . . FUCKED! I ended up in a weird dead end that was a small courtyard. I looked left. Nothing but building; to the right, nothing, and then I saw a garden with a low clear plastic cover, about twenty square feet. This was probably a protective layer someone had put on to prevent frost. I ran and dove and crawled under the cover.

Have you ever tasted heart? That's what I did that night. My heart was in my mouth. The wind whipped the plastic and made a rattling sound that was unbearable. Then my worst possible fear was thrust upon me. I heard a slamming door and running footsteps that got louder and louder as they approached. Getting louder, closer. Heart tastes bad. Can't breathe. Then in a moment of deathly silence, there came an eerie sound. Click.

It was a flashlight. It was illuminating and methodically scouring the dead end, all around and right onto the plastic. Momentarily, everything seemed to be bright. Then everything went dark. Then silence. How long I waited? I am not sure to this day. But I couldn't take it. It had been so long just lying there, my heart tasted so badly. Finally, I broke. I decided to give up and suddenly jumped up. "OK, sorry, I surrender!" My hands were in the air. How long I had been there, no one knows. My eyes looked around in the dark area. There was no one there. I slowly walked forward, apologizing and saying I give up. By the time I got to the street, I realized that I had another story to tell. I was on my way home. Selfishly, I did not go around the corner to see what happened to my friends. I headed home. When I got there, my housemate opened the door and said, "Hey, you and your friends keep it down, I have an exam tomorrow!" Ian was ranting again, complaining about my friends and his mother's plant. I was surprised to find everyone there. Everyone was happy and they were happy to see me. We were all happy. But there was something wrong. "Hey, where's Henry?"

"Henry got arrested!" The group chimed in together, "When you said run, we scattered like the wind, and Henry dove through the cedar hedge only to be stopped short by a chain-link fence." After some discussion, we sent a representative down to the jail. Fortunately, they found that Henry hadn't ratted and was subsequently released by 3:00 a.m. It was just in time for one more beer and the last night of school. It's no wonder I have recurring dreams about school.

Years later, I bumped into Henry at the post office in Oakville. My first memory of school was that night. Oddly enough, he did not remember anything of that night.

A graduate geological engineer
specializing in geophysics

Adventures in Exploration
My First Summer of Exploration

I had applied to a number of mining and oil companies for a job in exploration. Hmm, why did I not catch on right from the beginning about the mining industry? News of my first job in the exploration industry came from a couple of people. Initially, my friend Scott reported that, regrettably, someone had called to let me know the job was gone. Then, later that night while I was explaining my job woes to some friends, Pete, another housemate, interrupted and said a fellow called and said ignore the first call, I had got the job. At the time, it was good news. I had a job. Within three weeks, I was on my way to Vancouver, the head office for Anaconda Canada Exploration.

On the flight out to Vancouver, I sat beside a fellow who claimed to be the original drummer from the Guess Who. He said he left or was booted out just before they got famous. He was now working as the Western Canadian artistic director for a large Canadian chain store. He drank volumes of liquor. When we arrived, he insisted that he give me a ride to downtown Vancouver. After picking up our luggage we met his wife and child, he continued to talk to me like I was his best friend. When we got to the car he told his wife to get in the back and despite my protests he insisted that I sit in the front. We hopped in his Volvo station wagon. After running across someones lawn in order to avoid a red light and about halfway to downtown, his daughter, who was about nine years of age, piped up. "Mommy, is Daddy drunk again?" We barely made it alive to the hotel.

Following a brief introduction to the people of Anaconda Canada Mineral Exploration, I was told I had five days to kill in Vancouver. The secretary and some new colleagues took me on a tour of the back rooms of Vancouver. On my second night in town, I randomly met Yarmo Yalava who was sitting on a corner playing guitar for money. It seemed almost impossible, but I knew Yarmo. While in high school, one summer job had me on a peregrine falcon reintroduction project in Algonquin Park. Yarmo and I had spent half a summer together. The first thing I asked him was to play "Ready to be Canada Packed," a song he had written about chickens that I had remembered from the summer we had worked together. He laughed and I said, "Forget the street and come with me." We bought some beer and headed to my room on the twenty-ninth floor of the Blue Horizon. Yarmo had a long shower. We talked and caught up and he played guitar. I let him sleep on the couch and gave him $50 in the morning after breakfast. I haven't seen him since.

After a week of first aid training, survival orientation and geochemical sample training, myself and another student, a girl from Ottawa, jumped in the Suburban, and headed up the Fraser River to Hope and then to Princeton. We would be working out of a cabin about halfway from Princeton to Penticton in a place called Osprey Lake. The project was a copper/molybdenum property that was to be drill tested by a percussion drill. My job would entail walking through the woods, taking soil samples for most of the time with some geological prospecting, stream sampling, and helping on the drill thrown in.

The first part of the summer was spent on the Spring claims just up the road from the camp at Osprey and then we were to move over to the Hed claims to soil sample and locate drill targets. The project boss was Andris Kikauka, a formidable old-time hard-core Latvian geologist prospector. Andris had an old-time air, but was only four years older than myself. He liked eating foam rice crackers for lunch and expressing nonsensical views of the world that seemed to have some fit from time to time. Andris had true company grit and was determined to find something. After a month of hard work, the summer appeared to be going by without much of a hitch. We had a couple of stuck trucks and some cold wet experiences. Andris managed to arrange some really neat rafting trips down the Thompson River and the Tulameen and Similkameen Rivers. Overall, it was very exciting.

Finally, it came time to move over to the Hed claims and the drill crew was to arrive shortly and begin drilling. They were already thirty days late for the scheduled eighty to ninety-hole drill program that was to end in mid-September. I kept hearing the name of the company, Lorne Spence Enterprises. Soon Luca Riccio, the big project boss from Vancouver, would come up to the project to assess the situation. When Luca finally arrived, he would always have something to say about this Lorne character. It seemed Lorne had a trail of stories following him.

When we first got up to the Hed claims area, we found a campsite near a small lake at the back end of a large gravel pit. We noticed a trailer parked on the other side of the road from the gravel quarry and went to see if it was okay to camp nearby. The people in the trailer were also waiting for Lorne. Art was the cat skinner who was to fix the drill roads. Apparently, he had had to fix the cat himself, an old 1940s D6, and was waiting on Lorne to collect his month salary and his costs on the repair of the cat. There seemed to be early issues with this suspicious Lorne character.

The camp was small. Three of us were crammed into a sixteen-foot trailer among the pines. Work was going fine; suddenly another trailer appeared with three people just across the creek. It was the arrival of Lorne Spence and Co. Included was Ron, the city slicker nephew, whose father was tired of having him in the way and had sent him to learn a thing or two from Lorne. Ron was a big burly guy of about twenty-eight with an open shirt and big hairy chest with a gold chain the size sported by Tom Jones. Then there was Jim. Jim was a self-proclaimed driller from a small coastal town of Western British Columbia who always would be talking about the thousand feet he had drilled up at Keno Hill in the Yukon and how he couldn't wait to get drilling here. Lorne was to show up the following day with a large flatbed transport and the anticipated percussion drill. Ron and Jim seemed like pretty good guys, but both seemed greener than me and I was a true greenhorn to this exploration business. I must say that I was learning quite quickly that you had to be very careful in the bush because the smallest mistake could lead to a lot of lost time or worse yet, getting lost.

On the topic of getting lost, I had a close encounter during my first week on the job. Andris Kikauka, the senior geologist, had dropped me off with a tiny sketch map and some coordinates and bearings and distances with some instructions like "just go up that road and hang a right." I had failed to really get a clear idea of which little road I was to make my turn on, but did not want to hang around like an idiot. This was pre-GPS exploration, so compass and the sketches would have to do. I had a "hip chain," which was a counter attached to a ball of string so I could see how far I went. I should have wondered and worried a bit when the string ran out. I kept on walking a bit and realized I better go back. As it turned out, I spotted five drill holes miles from where they were supposed to be and nearly got lost. At the end of the day, I walked for what seemed like hours toward a road I never would have found. Finally, I ended up turning around and retracing my tracks to the main road where I had started. From my memory of the problems finding the road, we were able to deduce that I had put the proposed holes in the wrong spot. (Those holes were never drilled. If they were, who knows, perhaps a new mine would have been found. The industry has a good track record on lucky strikes.)

Later that summer we moved up into the area, and that's when Ron Savage, the driller's helper did get lost. It was a real scare, with over fifty people from the local communities involved in the search. In the end Ron walked out of the bush and into camp himself. At the time an RCMP officer was taking pot shots at a marmot on the other side of the small quarry where we were stationed. Ron came running out in shock, fear and anger as some of the bullets had apparently whizzed by his head.

That Looks Like Gold!

Later in the summer, the drilling program was underway, Lorne Spence ran a haywire operation with an assortment of characters making up his team. More often than not, the impressive-looking tank-mounted drill painted with fresh yellow Caterpillar paint was broken down. Lorne was always heading back to Vancouver to pick up parts, or get his oil changed. That was a more likely story. One time, he left Ron (his nephew) and Jim, a one-time blast hole driller, to finish the hole. As he left he said "Do not move the drill when you are finished this hole" Sure enough Jim thought he could move it to the next drill hole location. I thought to myself that it might be a mistake. The drill really worked well only under Lorne's command. The giant track fell off when he attempted the turn. Lorne was furious when he returned. He then left again to find more parts.

The percussion drill was a means to retrieve samples from the subsurface. The drill would turn and hammer down into the ground at ten-foot intervals, a stream of water would be sent down the center of the drill rods forcing the ground material up and out a spout. The water would fill three large pails. It was my job to pour the buckets out and sift through the material, bag the samples, and prepare them for analysis.

The young inexperienced driller had, like me, watched Lorne put his hand in the spout water periodically to check its content. Jim followed the same practice. Then on the day after Lorne had left the site, I noticed a lot of commotion between Ron and Jim as they were looking at Jim's hand. I had been dozing by the tree, waiting for the third bucket to fill. They signaled me over and started pointing. Jim was looking at his hand and pointing and yelling at me over the racket of the drill, "That looks like gold." Right away, I realized why Lorne had been paying attention to the water. I yelled back, "No, it is brass." "What?" They yelled. I yelled again "BRASS"

Within two seconds of my exclamation, the brass drill part that was wearing away rapidly in the drill somewhere caused the top of the drill to pop and go flying off into the woods with a swoosh of whistling steam and a large banging/clanging noise. Suddenly, there was silence in the woods. I pulled out my earplugs and watched as Jim fell to his knees in tears, crying out that Lorne was going to kill him.

Andris Kikauka, Ron Savage, Lorne Spence, and Jim at the percussion drill mounted on an old Sherman WWII tank.

When Lorne returned to the camp several days later (all attempts to contact him in Vancouver had failed), he was livid and threw a giant wrench at poor Jim. He got back in his truck and headed off back to Vancouver to get some more parts and a new drill head. I was back to prospecting and soil sampling duty. The rest of the summer had a few more interesting escapades including "Rob Gets Arrested," but I am saving that one until my kids are older.

A Cougar or a Bear?

A year passed, and a second summer job was achieved with Anaconda, a Canadian Mineral company based out of Vancouver. Our first base was living in an old house in Britannia Beach. Early in the summer, my partner, Trevor Boyd, and I, were sent up a major drainage system east of Squamish. The task was easy: we were to collect stream sediment samples from the center of all creeks draining into the major river. Samples were to be taken one hundred meters up from the mouth of each creek and then subsequently at 500-meter intervals up the creeks. Most of the lower points could be accessed with a truck, but the logging roads were not extensive, so we often had to get out of the truck and clump up the creeks. The whole project was about a week in duration. We worked as a team for safety reasons and to carry the samples, which were quite large. The samples were collected and sifted through special metal sieve nets so that the statistics could be accurately assessed. The company was focused on looking for a large copper discovery.

On the third day, we stopped for lunch and gazed out over the valley. There, way down in the creek, was something large and black. It was a huge bear. It looked ferocious. We briefly commented on the giant size of the bear, mentioned how we were glad we were way up the hill today and not down in the valley. We carried on. On the last day, there was pressure to get the last six samples, so we worked hard. But when we got to the sixth station, we discovered that there had been a snowslide, and the snow had slid all the way down the creek, stopping just above a sample we had taken earlier. There was no way to get the last sample. So we left the area, missing only one sample. In the following weeks, the crew focused on another project and we left the immediate vicinity for a month.

Returning a month later, the big boss, Luca Riccio, showed up and he was very excited. We all met in the office while he unrolled some new maps that he had brought with him. He was commenting on some great results from the stream sediment sampling program. He motioned us to look at the maps, and we saw some very unusual results on one particular creek. Then he started to follow up the creek and say, "See, SEE! THE VALUES KEEP GETTING BETTER AND BETTER, BUT LOOK, RIGHT AT THIS KEY SPOT THERE IS NO SAMPLE." Trevor and I looked at each other as we quickly remembered that that was the spot where the snowslide had been.

Luca said there was a lot of interest here, but that they needed to get that missing sample. He commented, "That sample could be the most critical thing done this summer." Everyone looked at me. Then, without much circumstance, came my mission. This mission did not come with the famous *Mission Impossible* saying, "Should you choose to accept this mission." No, it was my task. "Tomorrow, Rob, you need to go back there and get that sample. The rest of us are going to tour the old mine site at Britannia Beach." *Rats*, I thought, *I really wanted to go on the mine tour.* Oh well. The following morning, I packed my packsack, grabbed the truck, and headed out on the two-hour drive up the valley to get to the secondary creek and retrieve that critical sample.

As I drove, I started to think about cougars. There had been an attack a few weeks before, and it was slowly dawning on me that cougars could be everywhere and that I was alone. In fact, I was cougar bait. I drove as far as I could. Then I was going to have to walk up an old logging road, out of the trees, and into an old cutover. The banks above me on the road were almost six feet high. As I walked along, all I could think of were cougars and how they were going to pounce on me. I walked on the downhill edge of the road. As I climbed higher and higher, the road emerged from the forest, and I decided to stop for lunch before I got to the stream location. As I reached in the bag, it dawned on me that I had forgotten the sieve. Wow, what a drag. I had a big plastic gold pan and knew how to pan, but that was going to take a while when it came time to take the sample. It would take forever to get the right amount of material, at the particular sample size, for the sample. I finished my lunch and got going again. When the road bent back inward again, I stopped and gazed out over the valley. "Hmm," I said to myself, "this is the spot where Trevor and I saw that huge bear way down in the valley. Wow, I am glad I am way up here." Then suddenly, without warning, I heard a loud snap.

It was right behind me. All I could think of was a giant cougar. I slowly turned around. There, on the upper bank of the road cut was the huge ferocious black bear we had seen a month before. I was so agitated that I almost pooped my pants. The bear was in a perfect spot to leap on top of me and eat me. I started to whistle and it cocked its head. My fists clenched out of fear, and I discovered the gold pan in my hand. I slowly bent down with my knees and with a great swing of my arm smacked the pan on a rock to make a loud bang. "Click" was the sound that came out as the heavy-duty plastic pan broke into four parts. The bear looked at me and the pan and then slowly turned and walked into the bushes.

I gathered up the largest piece of the pan and quickly started walking. I wanted to return to the truck, but I persisted and headed up the path to the sample location. With the small piece of pan, no sieve, and freezing cold runoff water, it took about two hours to get the sample. I told myself I had enough small fines material and headed back down the road at a very fast pace. I was relieved to get to the truck. I was more relieved when it started. When I returned, I was interrogated. "Why is the sample so big and why did it take you so long?"

Subsequent summers were also spent in British Columbia exploring various areas from the Wolverine Mountain Range to the Iskut River and down along the coast up the Jervis Inlet. Each summer was filled with a meriad of characters, fun and fond memories.

Glenn Nolan and Rob Gordon celebrate the end of a great workday in the coast range of southwestern British Columbia.

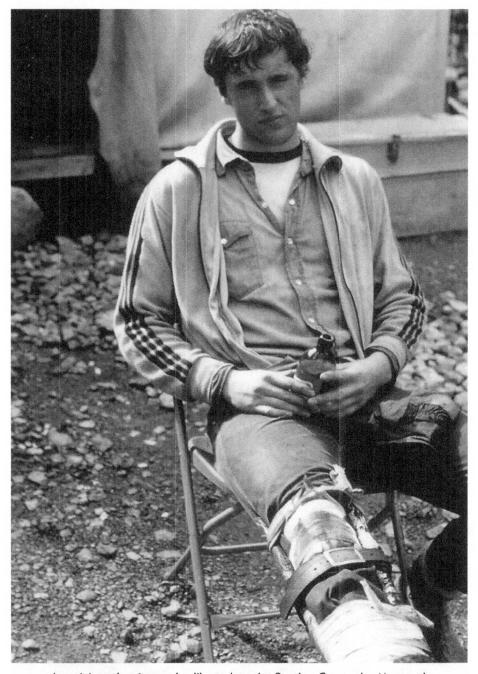

Imagining what it must be like to lose the Stanley Cup to the Montreal Canadiens, or the day I put a machete in my leg while cutting lines through the coastalmountain rainforest southwestern British Columbia.

Way up North

Work as a young exploration geophysicist means a lot of time out in the field. The year of 1986 brought me to Yellowknife in northern Canada. I was going to start working for a small geological consulting firm owned by a fellow named Lou Covello. Almost from the beginning of my employment, I found myself out in the wilderness, north of Yellowknife, collecting data. We referred to this aspect of our work as "out in the bush." We had projects all over the north, and we were introduced to all kinds of characters.

Initially, I spent about six months in a row working with a tall red-haired fellow named Gord Clarke. Gord was an ex-rugby player; we worked well together despite working in isolation for months at a time.

Gord Clarke and Rob, two Arctic explorers, April, Contwoyto Lake, NWT

On one of our projects, it was determined that the lakes had not enough ice on them to land a plane, so we would have to be transported to the remote camp on Cabin Lake with a helicopter. When we arrived at the airport with our boxes of food supplies, we realized that the boxes that were fine for the truck were not practical in the helicopter because they wouldn't fit. It was nearing the end of the day, so with no bags around, we packed all the gear loosely in the backseat of the helicopter. It was a Bell 206 helicopter, so there was plenty of room for the food. In addition to the food, we put a small generator in the back outside compartment.

It was pretty tightly packed when we finally left, but the one-hour flight was smooth and uneventful. As we approached Cabin Lake, we could see that the lake was black in color and the very thin ice was as smooth as glass. At the north end of lake was the camp that had been closed since the summer. We circled over the camp and looked around for a place to land. The pilot, Ian Campbell, wasn't happy because Lou Covello had assured him that there was a place to land behind the camp. Clearly, that was not the case. Then Ian muttered something nasty about Lou and circled again. In front of the camp was a small tee-shaped dock that jutted out into the lake. The pilot circled again and then said he thought the dock would have to do.

The shape of the dock was going to allow the helicopter to touch down on the tee portion of the dock with the front portion of the skids, but not the rear portion of the skids. This was going to be a bit dangerous, but not that unusual. The pilot commented that he would touch down and hold the helicopter steady with full power as he figured the dock could not hold the load. I was going to have to crawl out and crawl under the helicopter to get to the other side and open the door for Gord who was packed in with the food in the back seat. Once the plan was made, the pilot eased the helicopter into position. I waited until the pilot nodded and then I slowly crawled out.

It was difficult and a bit scary with the wind howling around the helicopter. When I got to the other side, I could barely see Gord, the food was all over him. When I opened the door, the food came first. It poured like grain from a grain elevator out of the helicopter and fell to the dock, the wind from the whirring blades, then grabbed it and scattered it like a fan. It slid easily, all over the thinly frozen lake.

Gord finally got out and I moved to the front of the tee-shaped dock to get out of the way. Gord then reached back and opened the back hatch. He slipped. As he fell toward the thin black ice below, he grabbed the back of the helicopters skid and hung on for dear life. That set in motion some near drastic events. Suddenly, the helicopter tilted on the dock and began to slide backward off the dock. I glanced up and saw Ian's shocked face as he struggled to find out what could possibly be wrong. As he got control of the helicopter and looked at me I signalled that Gord was hanging like a koala bear on the rear skid. He moved forward and allowed Gord to get off. He lifted up, turned sideways, and smiled as he saw all our food, including loaves of bread and small boxes of items scattered over one hundred yards of the lake. As he hovered away and the lake became silent in the November cold, we stood on the dock and looked in amazement at each other and laughed at our situation. It was getting dark and cold, and we needed to break into the camp and find the fuel for the stove and get set up for the night and then cook. That is if we could find any food. The temperature was rapidly dropping.

Our second night there, it was forty degrees below and our stoves started backing up. We were slowly being asphyxiated when I woke up. There was soot everywhere. I jumped up. "Gord! Gord! Quick! Outside!" For a moment, the two of us were lost in the dark. After we yanked the stove out of there, we spent about two hours getting resettled, shaking the heavy black soot out of everything. We deduced that the stove fuel started to freeze at thirty-five below, and the chemistry of the fuel going into the stove changed drastically causing the noxious fumes. Every night, it would drop to near forty below. The lake creaked and

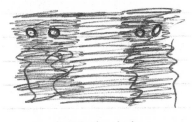

Lost in the dark

cracked, so we could tell the lake was freezing quickly. Within a week, we were able to retrieve our food and test the strength in the center of the lake. We were running out of heating fuel and would need a larger plane to bring some in, and it would have to land on the lake. We would need at least ten inches of ice before we could get the food, the fuel, and I thought it might be neat to go for a skate on the lake.

In the end, we were there for about six weeks. We heard a lot of wolves at night and often found large footprints on the trails that were close to camp. About three weeks into the project, it got fiercely cold during the day. The sky was gray and the temperature hit -42°C three days in a row. It became too cold to work; the second day, one of our wires for the geophysical gear rated to -40°C broke. It was a struggle to keep the tent cabin warm. Then on the third day, Rob had this crazy idea. I explained it to Gord, and he thought I was crazy. I said that years from now we would all have a laugh. I proceeded to tell him he simply had to take a few photos down at the lake. My crazy plan was to put my skates on and skate around with the geophysical sensor around me so that I could claim the title of fastest geophysicist. After much debate, we headed down to the lake. It quickly became a shouting match. I was yelling, "Take these pictures quick," and he was yelling, "This is weird." I said, "Trust me."

Gord Clarke and Rob Gordon, checking the ice thickness
early December, Cabin Lake, NWT Canada

Rob with Maxmin EM equipment, Cabin Lake, NWT. (40 C below)

The last photo has made it into a few of my presentations over the years when I am demonstrating how innovative the science of geophysics is.

Fastest Geophysicist in the World

The project lasted another four weeks, and despite nearly killing each other fighting over the ketchup one day, I think we managed some really good memories.

Wayne Kendrick, All the Way from North Bay

After Christmas, our first winter job was a large one, and we were slightly understaffed. I sent in a request to town via radio for two more people. With some help, I figured we might be close to finishing by the end of February. The next day, while out on the lake, I noticed a small plane circling above the frozen ground. *Great,* I thought, *my two new guys.* After the plane landed and took off, a Skidoo from camp came up with two people aboard. "Hi! I'm Francis Blackduck." "And I'm Wayne Kendrick."

Both Francis and Wayne seemed friendly to me. Wayne was six feet three inches and quite big. Our camp consisted of Gord, Lane Dewer, Roland Conrad, myself, and now Wayne and Francis. We had been listening to a couple of tapes in the camp at the time. The Eurhythmics and Paul Simon's "Graceland" as well as an Ian Tyson tape I smuggled in. One song on the Tyson tape was a song about Claude Dallas, a renegade bushman who killed two game wardens and had escaped down in Colorado somewhere. No sooner had Wayne introduced himself at the dinner table to the rest of the crew and started explaining how he had dreamed about coming to the north since he was in kindergarten and that all he wanted to do was fish all the time, when Roland, a local first nation who hated whites coming up north and "stealing" jobs, said that "Wayne was Claude Dallas and we should take him outside and tie him up." I grinned to myself. Wayne hadn't heard the Claude Dallas song. Roland then pronounced Wayne as Claude Wayne. An interesting four weeks passed in that camp with many interesting revelations about everybody coming to light. Roland was often quite outspoken. He was a proud Indian with a great sense of humor. Roland also liked his quiet times and when the job was over handed me a piece of paper saying he enjoyed the job despite having to put up with Wayne.

Pencil sketch by Roland Conrad.

The Shit, the Fish, and the Killing

Several months passed. It was February, and we were preparing for our first job in the barren lands in the winter. The initial plan was for Doug Bryan, Lou's partner, to come out and help for a few days. He was going to bring Mark Senqiuw to help lay grid.

The project was located in the Nodinka Narrows on MacKay Lake, high in the Arctic. An ice road to a remote northern mine was used to travel the 150 miles out into the barren lands to our site at Mackay Lake. The drive took six hours and was one of the most beautiful rides I've been on. Starting in Yellowknife the ice road was broken by portage roads that went between the lakes. Initially, we were in the trees, but as we drove on, the trees kept getting smaller, until finally, there were no trees. The land was pure white, the sky bright blue. It was February 10.

We drove onto MacKay Lake and then about halfway up this immense lake, we took a left turn onto a spur road that wound up to the old MacKay Lake mine. We drove right into a spot called Nodinko Narrows that split two large bodies of water in the northern part of the lake. It was after lunch sometime when we unloaded the trucks and started constructing the tent frames. The location of the camp was unique as it was situated in the middle of the lake to allow easy access to the grid area, which covered an area stretching across the narrows. Within three hours, we were inside having a hot cup of coffee. The oil stove was working well for heat.

I distributed various tasks such as setting up an outhouse and putting up an antenna for our communications radio. Wayne was already talking about fishing, so I assigned him the job of digging a water hole. He was thrilled. This job is usually a bad one because it takes hours, often with little or no sign of progress. Wayne was outside, lickety-split, with the manual augur. Half an hour later, he came back in with a stunned look on his face. "The auger won't go any farther, and I still haven't hit water." Roland laughed. "This is the north, Claude, not the south, the ice here is twenty feet thick. Now get back out there and keep digging! Do you want to catch the big one or not?" With a bewildered look, Wayne went back outside.

About ten minutes later, I stuck my head out of the door, only to see Wayne quietly sitting beside the hole, starting to freeze. I put on my parka and headed outside. "Wayne, you've always got to keep moving. You're going to have to chop a huge hole with an axe and shovel, and try the auger again when you get down farther." Then I said, "Now get to it, supper is in an hour," and I walked inside. Roland was shaking his head. "I knew I should have killed him on the last job."

After supper, I went out to see how Wayne was doing. He had a four-foot square hole, down about five feet, and was muttering and complaining to himself. "There's no water here," etc., etc. "Wayne, grab the auger again, you're almost there." Down he went with the auger. Finally, he hit slush and water started flowing up. "Get out of the hole." Wayne was now standing beside the hole as pleased as punch. He ran inside and reappeared with a hook and a bunch of line and promptly set up a line down the water hole. "Time for bed, Wayne."

The next day, work started on the grid. Three teams of two laid the grid. When we arrived back, Wayne was sitting out by the hole. "No white man from North Bay will ever catch a fish in this lake and live to tell about it," yelled Roland. That night, a storm blew up. The stoves were cranked full, but the winds howled through the tents and frost started growing on the walls. Everybody went to bed early to keep warm. Our tents were the warmest haven for hundreds of miles. Doug, Mark, and I were in the smaller tent that we set up directly on the lake ice with a canvas floor. This turned out to be a big mistake, which we later regretted because at night the cold radiated up from the floor and chilled the underside. We should have left a layer of snow on the ice to act as an insulator.

The third morning, I was particularly cold, with a frostbitten nose. I walked over to the other tent. Wayne was up sitting on his cot. He seemed pleased to see me. "Put the coffee on, Wayne." Wayne jumped up and started fumbling in the kitchen area for the coffee. I stepped outside and checked the thermometer: -38°C, and the winds were still howling from the northeast. The ice road had blown in. Soon the coffee was brewing and the aroma filled the tent. Roland and Lane were up. Doug and Mark were cooking. Shortly after breakfast and a second cup of coffee, nature called. I peeked out at nature; it was cold and windy. I didn't relish the thought of finding the outhouse. Throwing on a parka and boots, I ran out into the frozen hell. Over the bank and onto the road, I was surprised to see no outhouse and barely any road. I searched in vain for a place out of the cold to quickly do my pending duties. Suddenly, I noticed the truck. I ran over, lowered my pants, threw off my parka, and started to freeze. I grabbed the door handle and finished as quickly as possible. The tissues blew off in the wind as I ran back inside. "Holy cats! That's f—— cold," I yelled. Everybody laughed. I sent Roland out to fill and start the Skidoos. By 10:30, we were all outside. The wind was blowing hard, but the sun was shining. The day was memorably freezing.

It was good to come in at the end of the day, drink some juice, and relax. I wandered into my tent. Doug and Mark were sitting on their bunks. They were cooling their windburned faces by drinking a beer. "Have a beer," Doug said. I opened the can and chugged back half. "That was a pretty wild day," I said. "It sure was. Rob! I'm really upset, those guys of yours are total barbarians. I'm disgusted. You're going to have to teach them a thing or two. You'll never guess what one of those barbarians did." I could tell what was coming, so I quickly chugged back the other half of my beer. I could also feel my face turning red. I hoped it looked like windburn. Doug was no longer looking friendly. His actual anger was showing. Doug is one who never gets upset, so I was quite surprised to see his reaction. "Someone," he said, "someone shit in the middle of the ice road, and it looks like they never even cleaned themselves! Disgusting! Gross! I'll bet any money it was that Wayne character."

"You mean Claude," Mark added and chuckled. "Rob, you're going to have to talk to those guys. Right now!" Doug commanded.

The Lie

I said I'd take care of it and stomped out of the tent. I wasn't quite sure what to do. The sweat on my face was quickly starting to freeze. I threw the door of the kitchen tent open, and standing in the center of the tent, I bellowed, "Wayne!" Wayne looked around with his slow manner. "Don't ever, ever shit in the road again. You'll have to clean it up tomorrow. Doug was pretty mad with you by the way." I stepped outside. *Hmmm, that was pretty easy,* I thought.

The Truth

"Well, Doug, I hate to say this, but I'll take the blame." Doug looked at me with an astonished look. No more was said, but I knew I lost some points in Doug's book.

The next day, Mark and Doug packed up and headed back to town with the two trucks. The weather improved, so we had a week of good weather. Every night, Wayne went out to check the fish hole, and every night, Roland would say, "Claude, where's that fish? You would have starved to death by now if you were out here by yourself." Wayne finally spoke up. "There aren't any fish in this lake. If there were, I would have caught one by now." Wayne had been quite upset for a few days now and had actually been getting a little ornery just because he hadn't caught a fish. "Are you calling me a liar, Wayne?" Roland said. "People have died for less. Of course, there's fish in this lake. They can just smell the bait of a white man from North Bay!"

"Well, uh, I, uh, didn't call you a liar, but usually I can catch a fish," moaned Wayne.

"Well, this isn't usual, this is the NWT and your North Bay ways don't work," countered Roland.

Roland Conrad, MacKay Lake, February 1987 (note gun on wall).

The next day was uneventful, but at 5:30, Wayne put his head in the tent, and with a large smile, he proudly proclaimed he had something on his line. Everyone rushed to the door and peered outside. Wayne was bent over the ice hole, starting to pull in his line. There was a general feeling of admiration for Wayne by the remaining three of us. A half hour later, the sun was nearly set and a fierce wind was blowing up. The temperature outside was -35°C. I ventured outside to see how Wayne was doing. Grabbing a flashlight, I was astonished to see Wayne with just a shirt on bent over with one hand scooping the slush out of the water hole, which was constantly freezing as I watched. I ran inside and grabbed Wayne's parka and mitts. I felt nervous holding his line while I was yelling at him to put on his coat. I feared losing his fish. Heading back inside to warm up, Lane asked how he was doing. Roland was cleaning his gun. "I think he has it almost to the hole, but there is a chance it won't fit through." Roland spoke up. "Well, Rob, this is it. I'm going to shoot Wayne. No one will ever find his body and I'll be rid of him once and for all. Today, he said he liked my sister. I could never let him marry into my family. I just can't take the risk." Roland put his gun together and attached his clip. "Ten shots should finish him, although the layer of dirt on his skin will probably deflect a couple of shots, so I'm using armor-piercing bullets." With that, he stormed outside. Before I could do anything, ten to fifteen shots were fired right beside the tent. He came back inside with a big smile. "No one will find him. I rammed his carcass down the water hole."

I threw my parka back on and went outside to hold the light for Wayne. I could now see the large fish just below the hole. "I can't get it through," he said. After several joint efforts, we managed to get it through and up to the surface. As Wayne pulled it out of the water, I cheered. The other two guys quickly appeared at the door to see this prize. It was a beautiful twelve-pound lake trout. I took a picture of Wayne, his smile and his fish standing in the frozen dark.

Inside, Wayne was now the hero of the camp. Even Roland congratulated him. I figured that Wayne had finally gained some respect from everybody. Wayne was now telling old fishing stories from North Bay and everybody was listening. He walked around the tent with an air of confidence.

The following morning, I could tell a strong wind was blowing again and it was very cold. I reached to the stove, turned it up full, and curled up in a tight ball to stay warm.

At ten o'clock, I ventured outside. It was -50°C with gale force winds. Surprise, surprise, it was another official weather day. The day was busy with domestic activities. Roland said he would fillet the fish and cook a special recipe.

Lane made breakfast and Wayne was mumbling something about the fish. At noon, Wayne mentioned that he was going to wash. Washing was permitted, but usually, people came in early, during a field day to wash so as not to create a scene for the three other members of the closely packed tent. In any event, Wayne had grabbed one of two basins that normally had boiling water in and proceeded to strip down and wash himself while standing in the basin. Lane and I were trying to read but were constantly distracted by Wayne's singing and his general hairy presence in our tent. Roland made numerous comments about how hairy Wayne was and changed his name to Sasquatch Claude Wayne from North Bay. He told him not to wander outside like that or he might be mistaken for a bear and get shot. Roland was now cleaning his gun again and checking the sights on Wayne. The rest of the day passed slowly until dinner.

Everyone was looking forward to the fish cooked up the "special secret native way." Lane washed all the dishes from breakfast and lunch. Soon the meal was ready. Beautiful large hunks of pink trout garnished our Melmac plates. We all sat down and dug in. The first bite was delicious. Suddenly, Roland yelled, "Wayne! Which basin did you wash in?" Wayne, looking stunned and guilty, slowly said, "The little one." Roland screamed, "No, you didn't, you used the big one." "I did not!" exclaimed Wayne. "You could never stand in the little one! You used the big one! You used our dish pan!" Suddenly, I stopped chewing and Lane stopped chewing as flashes of Wayne's hairy, hairy body crossed our minds and the dishes had just been washed in that basin.

Uck!

Rob running magnetometer surveys, spring of 1987, Contwoyto Lake NWT

The Jax Lake Bear

It was a late start for exploration work at Jax Lake, but the fall would be devoid of bugs, I thought. Following a futile search of the town for Fred Diamond-C, we managed to catch a late single otter. It was 9:45 p.m. and the sun still hadn't set. Following a noisy two-hour flight, we arrived. I quickly concluded that warnings from some people who had flown over the camp were true. A bear had in fact entered the front of one of the tents and exited out the side. We now had an extra door in the tent. At 12:30, the sun was just setting, although I found this phenomenon hard to distinguish from a sunrise. It was cool, and the cold had made me anxious for bed.

The following day, I surveyed the damage. Amazing! The bear had broken into a large box of dried and canned goods, chomped every single can, and had spread flour, pastry oil, etc., all over the inside of the tent. Included in my daily activities was a camp cleanup. I had hated that bear when I went to sleep, but now I seemed impartial. Mike Gladiolas from Giant Mines walked by with a dog on his way to the "Placer" camp. Wayne caught a grayling at 10:00 p.m. He seemed more than pleased as it was his first.

The next morning, I was woken to the sound of an alarm. I was still dozing, but Wayne had gotten up and was just leaving the tent. I slowly sat up in bed and was starting to look for my socks. Wayne suddenly reappeared with an astonished look on his face. *He couldn't have caught another grayling,* I thought. "RRRRRob, a grizzly bear is just outside, eating cans." I strained to determine whether it was a true statement. He was reaching for the gun. "Where are my shoes and pants?" I quickly pulled them on. We crept out the door and peered around the tent. There he was, a large barren-lands grizzly stood standing in the door of the tent that he had ripped up a couple of weeks before. It was a good thing we had cleaned it up as there was now nothing for him to eat except us. I thought that if we hollered he may feel cornered. A strange sensation came over me. I wanted to take a picture of this enormous beast. I crept back into the tent and grabbed my camera. I couldn't resist. By the time I was back by the corner of the tent, he was moving toward us. I brought my camera up and shot him. One picture.

Grizzly bear awakening, Jax Lake, NWT.

The bear heard the click and immediately leaped to the air and started pawing and sniffing. Wayne was terrified. Fortunately, when I grabbed my camera, I had also grabbed two large cook pots. I started furiously banging pots. The bear let out a huge roar just like on Grizzly Adams, and our attempts to scare the bear seemed to stall. It looked right at us and then it started to move. "Shoot!" I hollered. The gunshot seemed to help. The bear hit the ground and bolted just by us at a frightening clip. We fired off a few more rounds and chased it over the hill and watched as it ran across the open countryside. Upon reaching a safe distance, it turned, looked, and stood up. Then it disappeared into the hillside of bear-shaped boulders. It was incredible to see the speed at which it travelled across the tundra. "Where's my other sock?" I wondered.

Later on, the daily radio schedule at 7:30 p.m. sounded like this:

Jax Lake - Yellowknife
Yellowknife - Jax - go ahead
Any traffic?
Scared a bear out of camp
Is it going to cause any problems?
No, we don't think so
Where did it go?
We scared it toward the next camp north.
Weather overcast, intermittent rain, cool, and damp.
Jax Lake has no other traffic.

Free Stuff

The topic of free stuff goes back a long way; perhaps the earliest reckoning is another tale from childhood. This was a knock at the door; upon opening the door, my mother called me, and to my surprise, there was Johnny Luxton's mother with a wagon full of toys with little Johnny in tow. John was bawling his eyes out (a form of intense crying). His mother was going from door to door asking parents and kids if any of the loot of toys in the wagon belonged to them. She said little Johnny had picked them up or found them over time, and she was trying to find the rightful owner. All little children take things that don't belong to them from time to time, and generally speaking, their methods and tactics are innocent. What I reveal on the next few pages are glimpses into activities that were not so innocent, yet in hindsight remain mildly humorous.

Ragu and Irish Spring

In 1970, some marketeer had the brilliant idea to pick new suburban neighborhoods as a trial grounds for introducing new products to the market. Coincidently, on my way home from school, I noticed large clear bags on doorknobs with giant jars of red stuff called Ragu. I had never heard of Ragu before, but it looked yummy for an eight-year-old. I decided to collect a bunch of them and take them down the street and behind some fencing that we used to hide behind during snowball season. The next day, I told a few of my friends about my stash, and we got some spoons and headed for my little hiding place. We then each took a jar and, once opened, proceeded to eat the whole thing. Well, I know I didn't eat my dinner that night. Later, in the grocery store, my mother subsequently wondered why I kept asking for Ragu, something she had never heard of.

Well, this marketing style of campaign and the indirect results were probably fit for discussion on CBC's great radio show on marketing "Age of Persuasion". One thing for sure was they must have figured that was a good idea because about two months later, I found thirty-seven boxes of Irish Spring on my neighbor's doorknobs. When I came home delighted with my haul, claiming we would not have to buy soap for a year, my mother was in shock. It was a standoff until my father came home, then after dark, I slunk around the neighborhood slipping soap back on people's doorknobs, and placing it under their car wipers. It wasn't until 2000 that I became very interested in marketing campaigns when launching some very sophisticated technology to the mining industry. Although I did not hand out Ragu, I did have some fun sending customized presentations in view-masters to industry executives.

Bazooka Joe

Have you ever chewed Bazooka Joe bubble gum? Inside each pack was a small comic and a picture of a prize you could win. Well, when I was a kid, the prizes intrigued me. You could "win" them if you saved a certain number of the comics and mailed them away. The man with the parachute, the binoculars, the periscope, and the spy camera were great ones. The descriptions were so vivid, but the number of comics required was absolutely ridiculous and prohibitive. Three hundred and twenty-five were needed in some cases. Assuming two pieces of gum per day, I would have to chew gum for six months to have a prize.

Bazooka Joe comic, used by permission, Topps Company Inc.

So one day, I decided I could get the prize early by telling a little white lie. I wrote a letter. Being in grade four, I was crafty enough to write the letter with my left hand. This made my writing sloppier than my usual sloppy right hand. It went like this:

Dear Mr. Bazooka Joe,

I really like your gum and have been chewing it for a long time. I have collected comics since I was four years old, and one month ago, I sent all my comics to you. I am writing to ask if you have received them. I had asked for the camera and the periscope.

Signed, Robbie Gordon

About three weeks later, a large package arrived, much to my mother's surprise, and inside were two pairs of binoculars, a telescope, camera, and a periscope. Wow. I was hooked. Over the years, my writing improved, and I found that a simple letter was sometimes all that was needed to help extend warrantees beyond the natural life of some products. My free shoe collection has been almost countless.

IMPERIAL
OPTICAL
CANADA

214 KING STREET EAST. TORONTO, CANADA, M5A 1J8, PHONE (416) 362-2020, TELEX 06-219691, FAX 362-3075, CABLE ADDRESS: IMPOPT

May 5, 1989

Mr. Robert Gordon
131 Meadow Park Crescent
Sault Ste. Marie, Ontario
P6A 4H1

Dear Robert,

Thank you for your recent letter and photograph depicting your misfortune (fortune) which ever way you feel.

Your letter certainly made our day here.

Obviously your glasses were very high on your priority list and for that I truly thank you.

I hope now that you can see perfectly during your exploration work and leisure time with the replacement pair of sunglasses enclosed.

Please keep your faith in our Bolle Product, it is the best in the market place.

I look forward to your continued Support of Bolle Products, enjoy!

Yours sincerely,

Celia Warren
Sunglass Department

CANADIAN THROUGHOUT — THROUGHOUT CANADA

Building a Library

Come the mid-seventies, I was starting to get sophisticated. The next great thing I discovered was the Grolier book company. There right in the magazine was the ad about a great book set and the statement: *FREE, no obligation, receive the first volume free. Simply cancel at any time and keep the first volume, absolutely FREE*. Well, this was too much to refuse, so I signed up. Within a week, a package arrived for Rob Gordon and my mother was asking, "What is this?" Wow, my first book. It was *The Ocean World* of Jacques Cousteau, volume 1. What a great book. It was with some reluctance that I sent the card back that said, "Please cancel my subscription." I waited for another package. I was a bit nervous, but no more books arrived.

Nearly four months later, another flyer came in the mail, and wow, a new series was coming out. It was called *The Peoples of the Earth*. This set looked really exciting, so I signed up. Three weeks passed and voila, *Peoples of the Earth* volume A for Asia. It was very interesting, and so it was again with some reluctance that I filled out the CANCEL my subscription box and mailed it back. My mother was starting to get a bit upset with me, but I insisted that what I was doing was completely legal, and there was absolutely nothing wrong with this process. Again I waited, but to my joy, no more books arrived.

I did well on a project about some sort of fish, and my knowledge of some people from far away was increasing.

Several months passed and a new coupon appeared. *"Science and Invention, volume A, yours free, with no obligation."* My library was quickly growing, and the focus was volume 1 and volume A, and I had lots of info for all my projects. After about six books, my mother had become numb to the process. So when the next coupon came saying, *"Now, for the first time ever, receive volume A of the World Book Encyclopedia, completely and absolutely free, with absolutely no obligation to purchase any other volumes, simply fill in this coupon and get informed,*" naturally, I was thrilled. I had used the World Book Encyclopedia before, but they were so large, you were not allowed to sign them out of the library, so this was a great opportunity to expand my knowledge base. I would simply check the box and mail off the card. I did, and three weeks later, nothing. Hmmm, that's odd. Another week went by and still nothing. *Hmmm, this is not good,* I thought. We would be going away for the summer to the camp at Smoke Lake in Algonquin Park in one week. I was still looking for the first book as we drove away. Then, as most summers went, I forgot everything and just slipped away into summer dreams.

Driving home at the end of the summer was a bit of an experience. We would leave in the morning and try to arrive in the evening. Many occasions, we would arrive at midnight because we had a late start or my dad just had to go and do one more thing at the forestry station. This time, we were on time. We pulled up the driveway. It was always such an adventure to come home. The smells were different; the garden had grown so much. It was 7:00 p.m., and my father and I rounded the corner to the back of the house. "Wow," he said, "what's that?" There at the back of the house was a giant box; it was split and looked like it had been soggy, and it looked like it had been there for the whole summer. I ran up to it and noted the return address: Grolier Books. Arggghhhh. I pried open the box and a giant swelled moldy book fell out. Surprise, *World Book Encyclopedia* volume B, below it was C and the D part 1 and 2. Oh no. This was a disaster. Plus, there was a bill. DUE NOW: $396.

By the morning, my mom was furious. All my mother's warnings had come to bear, and there I was, totally busted. I tried a letter with my left hand: "Dear Mr. Grolier, there has been a mistake," but a new bill came in the mail. We sent the books back. But another bill came. It was obvious we weren't getting anywhere. Finally, my mother, who was now furious at this whole escapade, pulled out her typewriter, and wrote a letter: tap, tap, tap. She was quite fierce in her tapping and the letter was not long. She sent it off and turned to me, "Never again!" That was it, I do not have any Grolier books in my collection today; I think I gave them to my sister as Christmas presents.

Well, those early events were the start of a bad side career in looking for free stuff. I never really called it stealing; it was like "it was too old to be worth anything" or "I'm sure they would never miss it."

One Halloween

Halloween was always a mischievous time for me, especially around the period of grade 6. I belonged in somewhat of a gang. It wasn't really a gang as you see today but more a group from public school of closely knit friends. This particular Halloween we had a wonderful plan to get lots of candy for relatively little work. Being that we were disguised, we thought it would be relatively easy pickings to rob candy from smaller kids. Our plan was a fairly simple, one where we would hide in the bushes along the path; the first bunch of us would jump out and rob the little guys, and the second bunch would jump out and try to save the little guys. As there were five of us, it meant there would be a lot of confusion. In the confusion, we would all scoop up as much of the candy as we could and then run away with the rest of us chasing. It seemed like a foolproof plan. Well, that Halloween was one in which there were thousands of parents on the streets making it very hard to find reasonable prey. As a matter of fact, we were soon forced to go door to door ourselves to salvage what had turned out to be a discouraging night to say the least.

Nine o'clock was approaching, and our band of thieves was starting to split up. Now there were only three of us: Mike Jones, Dave Taylor, and myself. Suddenly, there in front of us was a little squirt with a huge bag of candy. No one was left on the street. I was a werewolf, Dave was an old lady, and Mike was a bear. We grabbed the little guy and scooped his bag and ran off down the street laughing. Then, a shout came piercing through the night. "I know who you are Rob Gordon!" The other two wanted to keep running, but I convinced them to stop. We returned the candy to the squirt that said that he was going to tell on us anyway, so to shut the kid up, we each gave him a bunch of our candy and told him it was all a terrible mistake. As the bear, the old lady, and the werewolf walked away with heads down, we could hear the little runt laughing.

Well, that was just about it for the night as the bear decided to hibernate, so we said good-bye to Mike. Dave and I proceeded down the path that we had spent hours hiding beside and preceded one more time around the block to collect the dregs of all the local candy bowls. On leaving one house, I noticed two witches coming up the street. "Quick, into the bushes," I motioned. We dove into the bushes right beside the driveway and were silent as the witches walked by and up the steps. We didn't move a muscle; we just waited until they walked past again. Then, suddenly and without warning, the old lady and the werewolf pounced and grabbed the two witches' candy bags. My! They had strong grips; I pulled violently but to no avail. From nowhere, a huge broom was swung by my head; I ducked, let go of the bag, and ran. As I turned, I saw the poor old lady get a closed umbrella right across the face. Next, he received a broom across the back, and finally, they jumped him and proceeded to beat him mercilessly. I saw David finally break free and make a break for it with the two witches in hot pursuit. I turned down a driveway and quickly disappeared into familiar backyards and made for home.

Surviving University on Ten Dollars a Week

So the years passed and I found myself at university. The trend of minor misappropriation continued. I have already mentioned the story of Ramsey the sheep and there were other seemingly innocent acquisitions. A few chairs, parking meters, barber poles, banisters, microscope cases, and a beautiful 1964 Hamilton Beach blender that had come to an untimely end in the geochemistry lab. (It had been used to stir soil samples till the blades had been ground off.) Surely, no one would want that!

As a poor student at Queen's, I came up with a neat way to get more out of our weekly grocery bill. It did, however, mean eating more broccoli. We used to add additional bunches into the bunch as it was paid by the bunch. The big pink elastics could hold up to three bunches. It must have looked bizarre at the checkout counter. The bunches of broccoli the girl tried to scan required two hands and were sometimes bigger than basketballs. We also custom-wrapped the frozen pizzas. All our pizzas were also double-deckers loosely held together by poor packaging. It all worked well until my housemate discovered my trick and was so fascinated by it, he promptly went to the all night A&P across the street and tried to put five frozen lobsters down his pants and jacket. Needless to say, he was gone sometime that night after he was caught and hauled off to jail.

How to Win Door Prizes

While still at university, perhaps my greatest near feat for obtaining free stuff was my very bold attempts to win public door prizes. One evening, I found myself going to Dunning Hall to see a movie. There was a university movie house that sponsored film and encouraged the quieter crowd to come out and enjoy film without having to go downtown. The film could be enjoyed at the reasonable price of two dollars. For whatever reason, I found myself one evening sitting about fifteen rows back. The place was packed. At the beginning of the evening, they decided to have a door prize draw, and all of our tickets had been ripped in half and put in a bucket on the way in the door. Before the movie got rolling, three of the organizers of the club got up on stage to do the big draw. The prize tonight was FREE season tickets to the movie theater downtown. *Wow,* I thought to myself, *this would be great, FREE tickets.* They reached in the bucket and pulled out a number, read it, and called it out loud, "23674." I looked at my ticket and it read 23755. *Hmm,* I thought. What a drag. They held up the ticket and called out, "23674." Then they called out the number again for the third time. Suddenly, it was obvious to me. This prize was mine for the taking. "I win." I jumped up and yelled, "I won, I won," and then proceeded to run down the aisle, making a lot of commotion and jumping about much like a contestant from the "Price is Right" show after Bob Barker called their name and told them to "come on down" I ran up the stairs and onto the stage and then ran across the floor to the two people on the stage and jumping about. I threw my ticket into the draw bucket!

The two people were shocked; they had not had the chance to verify the ticket, but what could they do. So they reached out and shook my hand and proceeded to hand me the envelope with the prize. Suddenly, from somewhere out in the packed audience, a small voice came, "Wait a minute. I have 23674." The whole theater went silent. Then as the chap moved forward, the audience got ugly. There were boos! And a few people threw red solo cups on the stage; I quickly bowed my head and moved to the shadows. I later came back to my seat only to be scowled at by the people who sat by me. What was I thinking!

So years passed and there I was, a responsible adult at the Canadian Exploration Geophysicists Ball in Calgary. Sitting with friends near the end of the evening, suddenly, from the speaker they said, "The door prize draw will now take place." A distant memory came up and swirled around me. I sat up and looked around. I wondered if my old unproven scam would work here. Should I try it? What could happen to me here if it failed again? I began to sweat with anticipation. After several prizes had been handed out, there it was again, "23674 is the lucky winner!" I nervously looked around and the crowd was blank, the faces of my colleagues were blank. I took a breath and tried it all again. "I won, I won, that's me!" I jumped up, and running to the front, I hopped about with my arms in the air, making a lot of commotion. I then clambered onto the stage. As I approached the officials, who seemed to be much more official than the two I had met back at Queen's, I bounced and promptly threw my ticket in the draw bucket. There was silence, and the faces of the organizers were grim. "Excuse me, you weren't supposed to do that." I said that I was sorry about that and stood dumbly by. I cringed and a cold sweat started to cover my body. I waited an eternity for that little geek voice in the crowd that would inevitably come. "Excuse me, I have 23674."

It didn't come and the perplexed bucket holders looked me in the eye and said, "Congratulations, you have won season's tickets to the Calgary Stampeders." Wow. I walked back to the table and handed the tickets to my friend Ptarmigan (a.k.a. Andy Williamson), whose house I had been staying at while in Calgary. "Thanks for the hospitality."

The Towel Story

To round out and formally put an end to these scoundrel tales of some bad habits, I will tell this final story that took place many years ago in Brazil. It has become the famous towel story. I had been traveling with a friend around Brazil in the mid-1980s, and upon my first night's stay, I noticed that the hotels of Brazil took great pride in supplying guests with premium custom towels for use while at the hotel. This first four-star hotel for instance provided a large and plush towel, it was embroidered with Hotel del Sur and had four big stars embroidered across the ends. The bath mats were equally impressive. Upon review of the situation, I realized it was a relatively easy task to call the front desk and mention in broken English/Portuguese that my room was missing a couple of towels. I would promptly bury the towels in the bottom of my backpack and graciously thank the maid as she brought up the new towels.

Once successful, I proceeded to implement my towel-collecting strategy on a broad regional basis throughout Brazil for my monthlong tour. I stayed in a variety of hotels from two stars to five stars in cities like Recife, Salvador, Fortaleza, Belem, and Olinda. All levels of hotels had really nice towels. One of the best sets of towels came from the five-star Hotel Manaus in the city of Manaus way up the Amazon River. My pack was getting so big and fat that I actually had to purchase an additional large pack that was strictly dedicated to the stuffing of towels. After a month, I had successfully acquired the absolutely best collection of towels available in Brazil.

I finally ended up back in Rio de Janeiro, and I intentionally found a hotel where I had not yet stayed. The first one had been a four star right on the Copacabana beach. It was a bit overpriced and the service wasn't great. Another hotel would provide an additional towel. My policy of trying out the various star categories had me checking into a three star on the street immediately behind the Copacabana beach. At check-in, I placed my passport in the hotel safe behind the front desk as I regularly did. When I arrived in the room, I went to the bathroom and grabbed the bath mat and a nice large plush green towel and stuffed them in the bottom of my dedicated towel bag. I then called the front desk and left a message with the clerk mentioning I would need a couple of towels as they appeared to be missing. When I returned to the hotel later that day, I noticed that the towels had not been replaced as they usually were on my journey. The following day, it was check-out time. I grabbed my bags and headed down to the front desk to check out. When I asked for my passport, the checkout clerk who spoke mostly Portuguese asked the manager to come out. I was surprised that the checkout was taking so long and now a lineup was building. The manager first said that there was a problem and could I come with him to the safe room. When we were there, he turned to me and said that he would be unable to return my passport until the room was fully equipped with towels. He then had the gall to openly suggest that perhaps by accident I had put them in my bag. I was furious and put up the best possible front. After five minutes of ranting and raving, I was exhausted and said that I would double-check, just in case. He suggested I take my bags back to my room to check. This I did. When I arrived at the room, the bellhop let me in. Four other people appeared and stood around. It was absolute torture. I tried at first to rummage for them discreetly, but couldn't find it and then to speed things up a bit, I started pulling towels out of the bag. The people were shocked. I think I had over twenty big fluffy towels to pull out. Finally, out they came. With a shocked look on my face, I proclaimed, "Wow, this is a big accident!" I sheepishly handed over the two towels. Down at the front desk, the manager handed over my passport and said, "Thank you, Mr. Gordon."

Life Stories

Sent to Mexico

In 1978, I was sent to Mexico for part of a summer when I was sixteen. It was intended to be a holiday and to visit some family friends. My dad felt guilty because in 1963, the year after I was born, my father had to go to Mexico for several months and he took my mother and brother, but I was left with my aunt in Toronto for safety. Years passed and finally my father decided I should go for a month and I was sent. At the time, I was a teenager and had recently suffered a little with acne on my forehead. It was never really that bad, but from time to time, it flared up. The week before being sent to Mexico, it flared up. I was rather dismayed, and after watching an ad for Clearasil, I was prompted to clean my pores thoroughly and buy some zit cream. I took a rough rag and scrubbed my head. I scrubbed so hard, I was bleeding. The Clearasil stung so much I had to take it off. By the time of my flight, the next day, I had a scab the size of a baseball on my forehead. I looked very scary.

In hindsight, it was a very scary adventure for me. But at the time, I was just a nervous teen with a big scab on my head. Arriving in Mexico City, the wait for the standby ticket was unnerving as the time of the flight was approaching, and I was terrified I would have to stay in Mexico City; I wondered where I might sleep. Then finally, the lady came and signaled me that I could proceed. Arriving at the gate, I noticed the crowd looked like classic banditos with slicked-back black hair and big stomachs and white shirts and ties. Some had cowboy hats.

The day was sunny, so my fears had subsided. After takeoff, I started to imagine what Durango looked like. It was hard to picture it as I had never been there and hadn't seen any pictures. I knew Oscar was going to meet me. Oscar was Oscar Zarzosa, one of the sons from the family my dad had visited in 1963. In the early 1970s, he had lived with us for a year when I was in grade 3. He had become like an older brother to me just as Andrew, my true brother, was off to university. I knew my fears would go away when the plane touched down in Durango.

I was situated in a window seat at the very back of the plane right beside the engine. A large man who didn't speak English trapped me in against the window. No one spoke English. After sometime in the air, I fell asleep. It was probably two hours later when I was awakened by the landing gear coming down. We were landing. I was a little disoriented and looked at my watch. My watch had stopped. Was this Durango? Hmm, it could be. I watched closely as the people got their stuff. I finally asked the guy beside me where we were. Blah, blah, Durango, Guadalajara, Mexico, blah, blah, he shook his head back and forth. I was confused. Perhaps it wasn't Durango. I knew it wasn't the first stop, but maybe I had missed one. Hmm. I looked out the window and read the sign that was clearly displayed on the front of the building. The sign spelled "G-U-A-D-A-L-A-H-A-R-A."

More people piled on the plane. The engines started. I turned to the man again and desperately asked about Durango, more confusion. *The sign must have been Spanish for Durango,* I thought. Finally, the plane turned and started down the taxiway. I desperately asked the man to let me out; he did and I then ran to the front of the plane. The stewardess was upset and concerned; I babbled at them and asked them to "let me off the plane." Finally, they opened the pilot's door and asked him to translate. He smiled and said Durango was the next stop. The stewardess smiled. Wow, what relief; I turned around and walked back to my seat. There were many faces looking at me, everyone was laughing. Needless to say, my Mexican trip was quite an adventure, giving me lasting memories.

The Second Meeting of Wayne Gretzky
(And the Meeting of Ronnie Hawkins)

The summer of 1985 had started on a sour note because the company I had planned to go to work for after graduating as a geophysicist, Anaconda Canada Mineral Exploration, had decided to stop operations. This was some foreshadowing on the mining industry and a bit of a sign on the shape of things to come in my career choices, but I really didn't notice at the time. I decided that a canoe trip might take my mind off things. After the canoe trip, I was lucky to land a job with Echo Bay Mines and was sent to the North West Territories to work near the Lupin Mine. I was now a junior geophysicist starting to learn the ropes. I spent my days within sight of the mine, carrying out several types of surveys looking for drill targets. The overall objective was to find another ore body near the existing mine.

Me, sitting on the tundra on a nice day near the Lupin Mine at Contwoyto Lake, NWT. The small black dots are swarming black flies. Summer 1985.

It was a pretty fun summer overall; the people were amicable, and although the mine life was a bit surreal, it was a good time. I was a big slugger on the Exploration baseball team and remember fondly hearing people say, "Backup, it's this guy again" when it came time for me to bat. Then, there was the day we got the big official mine tour and got to see a gold pour firsthand. That was fun.

Halfway through the summer, we got an official break. The company flew my bunkhouse mate, Brian Scott, and me to Edmonton in the company jet and put us up in an apartment. The plan was to experience the metropolis of Edmonton firsthand for seven days.

Ready to pound the ball off the edge of the field, Contwoyto Lake, NWT. July 1985, note the frozen lake in the distance.

We enjoyed a generally good time as "The Klondike Days" festival was on, and a popular area was roped off for walking and the pub life was very lively. I must admit that the two of us looked a bit scraggly with poorly grown beards and not much in the way of city clothes.

One afternoon, Brian Scott and I were sitting, drinking fine wine, and just enjoying a lazy day at an outside patio. Suddenly, I noticed a group of three distinguished people walking down the street. It had been seven years since I had seen Wayne Gretzky, and he had been the farthest thing from my mind. "Wow, look at that. That's Wayne Gretzky." Before Brian could see where, I had jumped up and proceeded to run across the street to meet Wayne Gretzky head on. He was walking with a couple of people who looked a bit like Messier and Cement-head Semenko. In the early 1980s, Dave Semenko was the tough guy on the Edmonton Oilers who was known for being Wayne Gretzky's bodyguard.

The two friends of Wayne noticed me as I approached in an excited manner and proceeded to stand in my way. I came barging up, saying, "Hey, Wayne!"

"Hi," he said with a puzzled look on his face. I was so excited. "Hey, Wayne, don't you remember me?" I exclaimed. He stared at me and said, "Ahh. Sault Ste Marie?"

"Ya, ya," I hollered. "Ahhhh, Sir James Dunn?"

"Yah, yah." Now I was very animated and must have really looked like a street person with my scraggly hair. "Don't you remember Mrs. Morrow's geography class?" Much to everyone's dismay, he said, "Nope, but how's it going anyway?"

"Good," I said. I tried a sentence or two to remind him of a few people that he might have remembered as well and then I just said, "Well, good luck and have a good one," and walked away. Crossing the street, I noticed the whole patio was staring at me. *Yup, I knew Wayne,* I thought to myself. Not very well obviously, but I still knew him. Back at the patio, where everyone in the place was staring at me in awe, Brian could not believe what I had just done and was just laughing with excitement. We had a few more drinks and then it was off to the rodeo show where Ronnie Hawkins was going to be playing a bit later in the evening.

Well, after the excitement of the day, I really wasn't expecting that anything out of the ordinary would occur. However, I was pleasantly surprised. At the arena, we sat in the middle of an audience of predominantly country music fans and had a good time listening to Ronnie Hawkins. Ronnie had been a

Kissing a freshly poured eighty-pound gold bar,
Lupin Mine, Contwoyto Lake, NWT.

mainstay in the Canadian music scene for years, and although he didn't have
a hit song in years, he had a following. His current album in 1985 sported
a great version of "Stuck in Lodi Again." When intermission came, Ronnie
and friends disappeared off the stage. Brian and I were left to drink draft beer
and see if there were any girls around in the crowd that might want to dance.
Well, I had to go to the bathroom, so I told Brian I would be back in five and
headed over to the washroom area. On my way back, I noticed a big fellow
standing with his arms crossed in front of a door. I hesitated a second while
I wondered what was behind the door. As I neared the door, the guard was

temporarily distracted by a pretty girl asking for directions, so I just walked to the door purposefully and walked in.

It was almost like being in Alice in Wonderland. I found myself in a short hallway with a door at the other end. I ran to the end and opened the door, just as the lug opened the door behind me and yelled, "Hey!" He was too late. I was through the other door and into a party! I wondered if the guard would follow me as I walked farther into the room. In front of me, there was a giant table with cheese trays and biscuits and a man in a suit asked what type of wine I would like. "White please." I smiled. With wine in hand, I weaved through the sophisticated crowd trying to figure out what kind of party I had stumbled upon. Wow, I wish Brian were here. I am sure he would like this.

I came to an abrupt stop. There, right in front of me on a couch in the corner sitting beside a pretty lady was Ronnie Hawkins. This was incredible. I walked over and stood there amazed. "Hello," I said. "Hi, there," he said. "Enjoying the show?"

"Oh, yes sir, Mr. Hawkins, having a great time. In fact, I was wondering if you could do a song that I was thinking of today. It is on one of my brother's old records." "Well, which one are you thinking of?" I struggled a bit and sputtered, "Ah, I think it goes, something, something, reason to believe."

"Wow," he said. "I haven't done that song since I did that album years and years ago. Unfortunately, the boys don't know that one." But he turned to the girl and sung a verse and a chorus from the song. It ended, "Still I look, to find a reason to believe!" The girl swooned, and I was flying higher than I had been in a long time. Ronnie turned to me and said thanks for reminding him of that, and I said thank you and have a good one. I gobbled my wine and shot out the door past the bouncer with a look of confidence that had the bouncer holding the door for me. Brian was a bit upset and said, "Where the heck have you been? The show is about to start up again." I said, "You are not going to believe what just happened to me."

The Meeting of Tom Jones

Many years later, I was in Calgary for a mining convention. It was a mineral show and I had hooked up with some people from Vancouver. As the evening slowly wound down, I found myself with a mining colleague named Jonathon George from Crystallex, and along with a few others, we ended up at the fancy hotel bar just at the north side of downtown. The bartender had called out, "Last call" and shut the door to the bar. Only our table of six revelers was left with an assortment of drinks left to finish. After another twenty minutes, there was some loud knocking at the barroom door. The bartender went to see what the commotion was and the hotel manager stuck his head in. We thought we were going to be told to leave. A moment later, the door opened again and in walked three people. The most prominent had a black T-shirt, a smart jacket top, and curly hair. He looked very familiar, yet someone I had never met before. The group went to the bar and sat on some stools engaged in conversation. A bit later, it was my turn to see if the bartender could give us a few more, so I sauntered up to the bar.

I could not believe it. Surely, that was Tom Jones! I went back and got Jonathon. When we returned, he was singing Welsh to the lady, who seemed to be the wife of his friend. It was amazing. I ordered a fine scotch and stood there listening from six feet away. Suddenly, Tom stopped and turned to the bar and ordered a cigar from the cabinet and lit it. He leaned forward and puffed. I quickly leaned to the bartender and ordered a cigar. "What type?"

"The same type," I said. As the bartender snipped the end for me, Tom Jones turned to me and said, "Need a light?" I said, "Sure!" I leaned forward and Tom Jones lit my cigar. Man, did I puff heavy on that one. What a thrill. I was embarrassed a bit to ask for an autograph, but he said, "No problem." I had him make it out to Bobby Orton and the Rurals, which was the latest rendition of my own band I had formed with my friend Don Wright.

Tom continued to sing for his friends, and we all had a great time. Later, as we all said good-bye, we wandered out into the street. I found myself alone walking down the street humming. These words had come into my head by the time I had walked back to the hotel:

I met Tom Jones down in that bar.
He said, "Son, you can be a star"
Get a guitar, learn how to play,
sing out loud and clear
Then he turned around and
this is what he said,
He said, "Why, why, why, Delilah?
Why why, why, Delilah?

Tom Jones autograph addressed
to Bobby Orton and the Rurals

When I got home and told my friend Don about it, he laughed. Then he mentioned that he had tickets to see the father of Bluegrass himself, Mr. Bill Munroe.

The next day was another adventure, only this time in downtown Toronto to see Bill Munroe and the Bluegrass Boys. Naturally, we had to go and talk to him after the show.

Don Wright, Bill Monroe, and Rob Gordon

127

On the Meeting of Ronald Reagan

So another hot windy day kept the survey crew from flying and getting the job done. My boss in Toronto was furious. We had been camped out in Sierra Vista, Arizona, for almost two weeks. We had completed the first six flights of the project in the first three days and just need two more flights to complete the project and move on. My Toronto boss at Terraquest, Roger Watson, brother of Patrick Watson, a former chairman of CBC and Canadian TV personality, just could not believe the weather could be so good and yet so windy we couldn't fly.

I guess a few words of explanation are required to provide some background to this story. One of my earlier experience gaining jobs after I had left Yellowknife at Christmas in 1988 was working for a small airborne geophysical company. My work assignment was a geophysical operator, and our survey platform was a small Cessna 206, which had been equipped with wingtip magnetometer sensors. The crew consisted of the pilot, Greg Haenni, who had dreams to fly for Air Canada one day, and the flight-path recovery person and myself. I operated the onboard computers and provided real-time navigation. In 1989, GPS was a new thing, and for most of my first year flying with Greg, I read maps and called out, "Left, left, or OK right, right." As I followed landmarks as we attempted to fly low level long straight lines in a grid pattern. The goal of these surveys was to provide a broad scale magnetic map of the earth that could be used for exploration and drill targeting for the mining industry. I also checked data quality and ensured specific projects were completed in a timely manner.

This project included several interesting components, which started with the most southerly line of the survey flying a ten kilometer long line right over the US-Mexico border, just south of Bisbee, Arizona. Bisbee was an old mining town where they had been mining copper in a huge pit. Our flying

Greg Haenni and Rob Gordon preparing for a survey flight

height was 250 meters. This was very low by any standards. Bisbee was just north of what was referred to locally as cocaine alley. As we flew our second flight, we were going back and forth north of the border at low level. At one point, we were going to be flying right over the small airstrip at Bisbee. Greg, the pilot, was worried and started to ask me to look out for airplanes that might be in the area and wanting to land. It was a dangerous situation, but the area seemed quiet. Greg kept saying, "Do you see anything? Do you see anything?" as we flew right across the center of the airstrip.

C-GUCE Survey plane, note magnetometer sensors on wingtips.

Then, out of the blue, there was a plane. I looked over and there was a LEAR Jet about 50 metres away. I could clearly see the pilots face and his aviator sunglasses. That was really close! Then I yelled, "There's a plane." Greg immediately yelled "where?" and swerved off line. After a few desperate calls on the radio, a calm voice said, "We are on your port side above and parallel. Can you please inform us what you are doing in the area?" After a quick dissertation on airborne geophysics, the commander of the Lear jet that must have been traveling at stall speed informed us they were narcotics drug team and had been informed that a suspicious plane was in the area. They thought they had smugglers when they came across a Canadian registered plane flying low and over the airport just a few miles north of the Mexican border.

With that flight over, Greg was stressed and asked to go back. We got back, and that's when the winds started coming up. We were staying at a small hotel in Sierra Vista, which had a pool and offered free happy hour from 3:00 to 5:00 pm. We used the afternoon happy hour to relax. The next day it was out to the plane first thing to get those last two flights done. Once airborne, it was obvious we couldn't stay airborne. The data was shaking and all over the place, and we could barely hang on.

So twelve days later, we were still there and wondering if we could ever leave. The boss called every day; we could tell he was pulling his hair out. He was getting angrier and angrier and was convinced we were just goofing off.

(We actually would give up at happy hour, but otherwise were on 24-7 notice to get in that last flight.)

Then one morning we got up and things were still, everything was calm. "Let's go." We raced down to the airport and were loading, doing the preflight walk around, and getting ready to go. The Sierra Vista airport shared a runway with the Fort Huachuca air force base. It was always fun to take off because it was so long and we seemed so insignificant. Fort Huachuca was the third alternate for landing of the space shuttle, so it wasn't unexpected to see all kinds of jets coming and going from the other side. But today, a medium-sized jet landed and piled up to the terminal while we were getting ready. Greg said, "Hey, look at that." In the distance, coming up the civilian road to the terminal was a parade of about seven large Suburban vehicles. The first one stopped, and three large men with sunglasses and cowboy hats got out and walked over to our plane.

"You are requested to leave your plane and get behind the fence immediately."

"But we just need to—," I proclaimed. Then the voice came forward bluntly. "You need to leave the area immediately and get behind the fence. The president will be leaving on that plane. Please do so immediately." We left and were in shock. Then, sure enough, there he was. That's when I recalled the news from a radio show a few days earlier and repeated in the *New York Times*.

REAGAN IS INJURED IN FALL OFF HORSE

By ROBERT PEAR, Special to the *New York Times*
Published: July 05, 1989

Former President Ronald Reagan suffered minor injuries when he was thrown from a horse in Mexico today, the Secret Service reported.

Stephen E. Garmon, deputy director of the Secret Service, said Mr. Reagan had been taken by a military helicopter to a hospital at Fort Huachuca, an Army base near Tucson, Ariz., where he stayed for about five hours.

The accident occurred in the Mexican state of Sonora, just across the Arizona border, where Mr. Reagan was on a hunting trip at a private ranch. "The extent of injuries was minimal, but to be

on the safe side he was taken to Fort Huachuca for observation,"
Mr. Garmon said. Horse 'Bucked Wildly'

In Los Angeles, Mark D. Weinberg, a spokesman for the 78-year-old former President, said, "The horse Reagan was riding bucked wildly several times on a rocky downhill slope and eventually stumbled," throwing Mr. Reagan.

A small crowd had gathered, but I was the only one who had a big old camera and started taking a few shots. What was really neat was that I managed to connect with Nancy Reagan for one shot, and I think she told her husband to wave at the guy with the camera for another.

Ronald Regan prepares to board plane

Nancy Regan connects with Rob the photographer

Nancy Regan tells Ronald to connect with Rob the photographer

So there we were, unable to fly. I managed to get a few pictures of the crowd, but by the time the plane left, the winds had come up again. I called back to the boss in Toronto.

"Hi, Roger."

"Hi, Rob, did you fly? I read the weather reports and it said it was calm down there today."

I replied, "Roger, you are never going to believe this."

On Meeting Phil Esposito or "I Won the Watch Story"

The stories in this book loosely follow a chronological nature. I had trouble with this one as it crosses several topical boundaries from "brothers" to "free stuff" to "life stories." I decided to put it here under "life stories." When I grew up in Sault Ste. Marie, there was a period when the famous Esposito brothers lived literally right around the corner from my father's house at 131 Meadow Park. They lived on Shannon Road. On occasion, in the spring and summer of the late '60s one or other of the brothers, Phil or Tony, would show up and there would be great excitement as the kids would run over to get their autographs. One spring, my brother sent me over to get Esposito's autograph. I ventured up to the side door and knocked. A very tall large man came to the door and asked, "Yes, may I help you?" At the time, I was at a stage in my life where I had been drawing and sketching goalies, so it was natural for me to know a bit about Tony Esposito. "May I please have *Tony Esposito's* autograph?" The tall man gave me a puzzled look and with a smile reached into a box by the back door where there appeared to be hundreds of pre-signed glossy photos. He handed me the picture and as I said thanks and turned to go, he said, "Maybe you want this one too?"

I gladly took the other picture, looked up, and said thanks! When I got home, I told my brother that the fellow in the second picture gave me Tony Esposito's photo. Andrew exclaimed, "You dummy, that was Phil Esposito!" Later in early high school, I had the bad idea to sell all my sports cards, hockey paraphernalia, and comic books so that I could buy a ticket to Alice Cooper. So I was left without Phil or Tony's autograph.

Years later, in January of 2007, an interesting opportunity presented itself in a full-page ad in the *Globe and Mail*. "Win a chance to meet Phil Esposito and other hockey greats and a $5,000 Swiss watch by writing a hundred words on why you like Copperhead Beer and why you should get to play hockey with the hockey greats." The ads on TV had the president of Copperhead in the locker room with the likes of Tony and Phil Esposito, two Sault Ste. Marie hometown boys who had famous and storied hockey careers. I pondered how I could come up with a solid hundred-word winner. A week passed and I still could not formulate a winning entry.

Then one day. I received an e-mail from my brother. It had an attachment that my brother wanted me to read. It was a story he thought deserved to be in the book I was writing. My initial thoughts were that it wouldn't belong. But after reading it, I thought in a roundabout way it could fit into the book. In fact, I almost felt like the Grinch when he first had his big idea to stop Christmas. Not that it was an evil idea, just that it was such a good idea that I had to set a plan in motion to win the prize. A few other things might have to happen, but his story gave me the catalyst for my hundred words and I knew I had a good chance to win. The prize was a $5,000 Ernz Benz Swiss watch. The attachment from my brother was as follows:

May I Have Your Autograph, Mr. Esposito?
Guest Chapter
by
Andrew M. Gordon

I have bad circulation in my toes and fingers for one reason only: my father was the son of hardworking but thrifty Scottish immigrants. You know the type—the ones that invented copper wire by fighting over a penny. In the cold winters that were Sault Ste. Marie in the early 1960s, my dad had a choice to make. For $5, his son—me—could play hockey as everyone in the Sault did—indoors in the one City League arena. But for $2, I could "build character" and play outdoors at -40°C every Saturday morning in the Recreation League. Guess what? I still remember the cacophony of sound that came from us pounding our skates on the floorboards of the so-called warm-up shack between periods—a useless attempt to thaw out our feet ensconced in thin leather wobbly skates from Canadian Tire. I cried myself to sleep in my mother's arms every winter Saturday for three years in a row during thaw-out time—and to this day, can't hold a wrench outside on a cool autumn day. Thanks, Dad!

In 1964, I played for Gartshore Construction under a coach who liked to play his capable son in all positions most of the time. I scored zero goals, but once dumped an opposing player into a snowbank, thus allowing Billy Hollingshead a breakaway and his first goal—I guess that counts as an off-handed assist. In 1965, I played for Esso Fuel. A young but vocally French Mr. Paquin was our coach. We went 5 and 2 over the season, and I got three goals—apparently not enough to satisfy Mr. Paquin who, on both occasions of our losses, ordered me, a left winger, into goal. You win, you lose, as it happens.

Perhaps to warm his soul against the angst his young son was suffering in the Recreation League, my dad often came to the games where he was very careful not to yell at Mr. Paquin. He saved his most vocal criticisms for the parents of the players on the other team—the net result being an on-ice hammering of yours truly by their sons—resulting in more yelling and more hammering. You lose, as it happens.

There's no doubt that the Sault was, and continues to be, a great hockey town. Back then, the names of the local born boys on everybody's lips were Matt Ravelich, Matt and Marty Pavelich, Gene Ubriaco, Lou Nanne, Joe Klukav, Don Grosso, Ron Francis and the Maki brothers—Chico and Wayne, and of course the Espositos—Phil and Tony. More recently, as you've read in other chapters, Wayne Gretzky surfaced, and just a few years ago Ted Nolan then Islanders coach, and Paul Maurice then Leafs coach, went head-to-head. Back then, Bobby Baun and others would show up to the hockey banquets where we all listened to speeches and ate rigatoni—it was the Sault, after all!

And of course, we all collected hockey cards. Those from the other side of the tracks bought theirs from Sing Hong at the Holiday confectionary. Those of us not so lucky saved the backs of Cheerios boxes or sent coupons to the Billy Bee Corn Syrup Company. Word on the street was that two Cheerios cards equaled a normal store-bought flashy card.

The entire Cheerios exercise was one fraught with danger. The photos of the hockey players—the signed ones were worth a premium—were large and covered almost the entire back of the box. Getting them extricated from the back was the most difficult, especially since millions of Cheerios on the kitchen floor were frowned upon and usually resulted in grounding or some other punishment like having to finish our mashed potatoes.

Mom always went shopping on Friday night, and I had been warned one particular Friday—after five subsequent weekly Cheerios dumps—not to do it again. I waited behind the closet door until I heard her go into the living room. I made a mad dash for the grocery bags and grabbed the Cheerios. I just about fainted—it was Phil Esposito—unsigned, but nonetheless rare, and worth a lot. I brought my scissors up to the box and carefully began cutting, my heart thumping in anticipation of finally getting my hero. Halfway through the exercise, my brother, whom you've been introduced to in other parts of this book, showed up and did what he does best: "Whatcha doing?" Jab. Jab. Jab. Poke. Poke. The scissors swerved and RIP. More Cheerios on the floor, him scampering away, and me left in front of a frothing mom, scissors, and Phil in hand, standing in a pile of Cheerios. Grounded again, but I had Phil.

And then the collective gang on the block waited through the rest of the winter for the losers in the semifinals to send their Sault Ste. Marie sons home. We were vigilant, and if a Stanley Cup loser came home, we knew it. We paced and we waited.

One Saturday morning, halfway through Roy Rogers—on our seventeen-inch black-and-white—there was a bang at the door. Bruce Murray and Ricky Doan were hyperventilating on the front steps. "He's home! He's home! Get your card!" I was in my bedroom and out on the street with Phil faster than it takes to spill Cheerios, leaving Roy, as he always did, to fade into Sky King, the last of the silver screen cowboys (with a plane).

The Espositos lived around the corner from us and over a street. We weren't sure there was a Mr. Esposito, but we knew Phil and Tony came home to visit their mother. The ritual was this: we formed a long slow-moving line that walked up and down the sidewalk in front of the modest yellow-brick bungalow, occasionally glancing at the drawn blinds in the picture window. Occasionally, they moved, causing us great excitement. And finally, the side door would open and a voice would say, "OK, boys!" We'd make a mad dash for the door and form a squabbling, pushing, and shoving line.

This time, I was fourth from the front, out of breath, but knowing I was close to increasing my hockey card worth substantially. I glanced at the cards in my hand and then up and then down again in horror. I'd grabbed the wrong cards! There staring at me in all his Chicago Black Hawk glory was old No. 3, Pierre Pilote! Oh no! What to do! Run home? No.

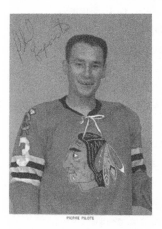

Phil Esposito Autograph on Pierre Pilote card

I'd miss my chance. But by then, it was too late. I was being shoved toward the door and the waiting was over. There he was, the (at that time) Great One! He was bigger than life—I timidly spoke, "May I have your autograph, Mr. Esposito?" "Sure, son, give me the card." I hesitated and haltingly handed it over. He started to write and then stopped, looking at me rather strangely. It was all a blur so I don't know whether I turned red, shrugged, blathered something, and closed my eyes or all four. But he sighed, signed it, and handed it back to me, looking at me like the idiot I was. I took the card and looked at the signature, hoping beyond hope that it was on my Phil card—but it was no use—all I saw was Pierre looking back at me.

There was only one thing to do—so I handed him the second card. This one really caught him by surprise, and he started shaking his head. Then he grinned and scrawled "Phil Esposito" on the top of Moose Vasco's head. I grabbed the card and

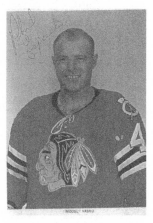

Phil's autograph on Moose Vasco card

then it was all I could do to run away in embarrassment.

I was the laughing stock of the neighborhood. After all

that, after being the first kid to get a Cheerios Phil Esposito, I didn't even have his autograph on the right one. But everybody else did—my card reputation and marketability were ruined, and I found myself on the losing end of many subsequent hockey card trades.

I could redeem myself though, and I put a plan in action.

 That fall, Gordie Howe came to town, and I got my mom to take Gord Burke and I down to the old T. Eaton store on Queen Street. We waited in line for a half hour and I got him. I nailed him. I got "Gordie Howe" on a Gordie Howe card. And that was just the beginning— before the year was out, I had personal greetings from Maurice Richard of the 64–65 Canadiens, Johnny Bower, Bobby Baun, and a host of others. I got my respect back—my trades meant something again, but I was still missing the Holy Grail, but not for long. I had a plan.

My dad had a friend who worked for the local radio station and who occasionally gave him tickets to the Hounds. In 1962, he had arrived back from a Stanley Cup series between the Black Hawks and the Maple Leafs and thrilled me by giving me the glossy gamebook. The cover depicted Bob Pulford rifling a puck past Pierre Pilote and Glen Hall into the net—it was one of my most valued not-for-sale hockey mementos. I dug it out and waited out the cold, lonely winter. I couldn't wait to see Phil's face when I presented it to him for signature in the spring. His signature gracing the front cover would make me the king of hockey card collectors in northern Ontario.

Well, it wasn't long before I was in line again at the Esposito's house, but this time, I exuded confidence—long gone was the trepidation and embarrassment associated with the Pilote-Vasco fiasco. I waited in line.

"May I have your autograph, Mr. Esposito?" I asked sweetly. He grinned and grabbed the 1962 gamebook. "What's your name, boy?" he asked. "Andrew," I replied truthfully. Quickly, he scrawled something on the front and handed it back to me. I thanked him and turned to go. He said, "Just a minute, son." I froze. "I remember you—you're the one who got me to sign my name to Pilote and Vasco." I panicked. You could have heard a puck drop. "It's OK. I cleared it with them, and they said it's fine!" I breathed a sigh of relief and started off again. "By the way," he said, "I didn't start to play for Chicago until 1964," winking at me. And so, once again, Phil had erroneously signed on top of Pierre Pilote.

It took another year for me to track something correct down, but as you can see below, we finally got it right! I haven't seen Phil in person since 1965, but my heart was there with him in 1972 during his famous rant at the Summit Series. And I'm glad to remember him as one who was patient with me—a true Great One from my hometown.

Phil Esposito autograph on Toronto game program

Phil's autograph on a Chicago ticket

After considering my brother's interesting story, I realized that my brother still did not have a picture of Phil Esposito, and he didn't really have a good Phil Esposito autograph. I decided that to complete my brother's story, my one hundred words would have to appeal to the judge's emotions in order for me to win the prize and then, perhaps my brother could get Phil's autograph in proper style. I wrote and planned on submitting the following;

100 words on why I love Copperhead
And why I should get a chance to play with Phil Esposito.

I love Copperhead. First, it is crystal clear, the color of fine whiskey. Secondly, it is smooth, like Don Ho's "Tiny Bubbles" song. Finally, it has distinctive and great taste. I am from the Sault and lived just around from Phil's parent's house on Shannon Road. As a young boy in the early '60s, my older brother tried many times to get Phil's autograph and, arguably, failed miserably. I would like to invite my brother to

141

the game to get Phil's autograph, and if there is room, let him play as well. It would be a birthday (51) present.

I also included the story my brother wrote as an attachment to my one hundred words. In addition, along with my submission, a beer cap was required.

I packaged it up, added a stamp, and sent in my submission. It was months till the draw, so I left it at that. About a month passed and my wife and I were visiting her cousin Andrea Drynan. Andrea had married Gord Ullman. Gord, son of Norm Ullman the famous Toronto Maple Leaf and Detroit Redwing, was mildly interested in my story of how I was going to win a watch, but being a lawyer, he commented that he thought that they might not just read the words, but rather just pick an entry from a bucket. As an expert on how things get picked from buckets, I realized I was going to have to step up my game and create more entries to increase the odds. I did and submitted about ten more entries. Then one day, I ran out of stamps, I walked across the street to the post office and asked for a stamp. The clerk looked at my package suspiciously and stated that it was too thick for a single stamp. He then proceeded to pull it quickly through a narrow slot that seemed to be a gauge. To our mutual surprise, the letter ripped and a beer cap came flying out and clinked on the floor. He said that the letter would not go through with a single stamp.

A gift from Norm Ullman

The next day, I was caught in the office pounding beer caps flat so they would fit in my next batch of entries.

Well, the months moved by slowly, the draw date was moved because Steelback would be sponsoring the Indy race car event, and the draw and prize were to coincide with the start of the race. It was now June and the draw date had come and gone. I was a bit upset as I really thought I had had a chance. We went to the cottage for the weekend. Upon returning, I listened to the messages on the answering machine. "Hello, Mr. Gordon. This is Frank Diangelo, CEO of Steelback Beer. I would like to tell you that you are a winner of one of fifty

Limited Edition Ernz Benz watches. The watch is valued at $5,000. Please come down to the Steelback Indy to collect your prize."

That was the entire message. I played it several times. At first, I didn't believe it, but after contacting the company, it was true. They would be handing out prizes at the Steelback Indy on the following Saturday at 2:00 p.m.

Wow. What a surprise. As a winner of very few things in my life, I was suddenly very happy. The next week, I was quite distracted in the office and kept thinking to myself, *I won the watch.*

What a thrill. My happiness was soon to abate when my wife informed me she wanted nothing to do with going to the Steelback Indy to help me collect the prize. Following days of begging, I was getting nowhere. I decided to call my brother and ask if he would come down with me. Well, at first he was quite reluctant, but when I said Phil Esposito would be there, he thought that it was a good idea. I continued to plead with Katie, explaining that it would be fun to see such an event and that Sophie, my daughter, would probably like the train ride to go downtown.

Katie Sophie and Uncle Andrew at the mini putt contest on race day.

Finally, she capitulated. On Saturday, we made ready to go downtown. It was a hot day. Andrew showed up and we headed off to the GO train station in Clarkson. What a surprise; we found a completely packed train pull in from the west. Not only was the Indy on, but also there was a baseball game at the Sky Dome. It was a muggy hot summer day on the July long weekend. We would normally be at Smoke Lake. Katie did not look happy when I grabbed Sophie and barged on the train. We ended up with standing room only on the top floor. As the train made its way into Toronto, each platform was jammed with people who could not believe how stuffed the train was, yet they all fit on. We were like sardines when a rumor went around that the train wasn't going to stop at Exhibition where the race was. Katie frowned.

When we finally arrived, it was quite interesting. We wandered around the grounds, looking at fancy cars and scantily dressed girls in Steelback bikinis. It was an eye-opener for all of us, but generally everyone was in a good mood.

Finally, it was two o'clock, time to get the prize. We went to the Steelback beer garden where Mr. Diangelo would be handing out the watches. Unfortunately, no children were allowed in the Beer Garden. This meant that Sophie and Katie would have to wait outside while Andrew and I went inside. We grabbed a couple of large Copperhead beers and went and sat near the stage. Suddenly, there was commotion near the side of the stage, and there stood Frank Diangelo and Phil Esposito! "Look, Andrew, there's Phil Esposito!" Andrew grabbed his camera and started flicking photos and told me I should head up to the stage.

Rob waving to Katie and Sophie, Mr. Happy guy! Waiting my turn for my new watch.

On stage, there were only eight of us to collect the prize in person. All of the winners were pretty happy. I waved to Katie, holding Sophie at the back of the beer garden. I could not help but wave like Richard Nixon "I am not a crook" with peace signs gesturing!

"I am not a crook!"

When Frank Diangelo introduced me, he said I was from Oakville. As Phil Esposito handed me the watch, we shook hands, and I yelled out, "I'm from the Soo!" At which point, he turned to the crowd and burst out laughing.

Rob makes the Espo Laugh

145

Following the ceremony, it was virtually impossible to talk to Phil as he was surrounded with people saying hi and trying to shake his hand. When I returned to the table, I said, "Let's go, Phil will be at the signing booth at 3:00 p.m."

When we arrived back, Katie look exasperated and Sophie was about to pass out. Katie insisted that we leave right away. I explained that Andrew had come all this way to get Phil's autograph. "Can't we just stay a bit longer?" I pleaded. "Absolutely not" was Katie's reply.

As we were walking towards the exit, we passed the autograph signing area. A large line was forming at the autograph stand. Not only was Phil going to be there, but also Dennis Hull, Eddie Shack, and Bob Probert were signing autographs. Andrew noticed that Katie was a bit tired of the noise and heat and said that he could get Phil's autograph some other time. But just then Phil arrived. He was going to be the last stop in the autograph line, but was standing right there, not fifteen feet away. I said to Andrew, "Quick, before they start the line just run up there and ask him to sign your story." Andrew said no, but Katie chimed in and said, "Good idea, quick, run up there." Andrew said, "You think so?" We both said sure.

By this time, Phil was sitting down and they were about to start with the autograph session. The line was now about two hundred strong. Andrew ran up to Phil, and we saw him pleading with Phil to sign his paper. Phil looked a bit agitated and was shaking his head. But Andrew wouldn't stop. He was over the edge, he thought Phil would break. Finally, as Katie and I stared on in disbelief, Phil stood up in front of my brother. He was talking sternly to my brother, then finally took out his large finger and poked my brother in the chest. Andrew came back to us with his head down and said, "Well, that didn't work." We asked him what happened. Andrew exclaimed "that he refused to sign and finally said, 'Listen, if I let you in front of these guys here, they're going to think I'm the asshole instead of you!' At which point, he jabbed me in the chest."

Katie was laughing by now and said, "Well, let's line up and get this over with." The line took quite some time, but when we arrived, Phil remembered us. And with a laugh said, "Not you guys again!" We revisited: the Soo, the watch, and Andrew's failed attempt to butt in line while sharing a laugh. Katie took some pictures. My brother was pretty happy, but I still don't think he got Phil's autograph on an actual photo of Phil. But by that time, it no longer mattered.

Andrew gets his autograph. Phil with his new limited edition
watch #7 of 50. An exhausted Sophie in foreground.

An exhausted family. Katie, Rob with limited edition
Ernz Benz watch (#38 of 50), and Sophie.

Now my family wants me to sell the watch and take them to Disney.

On Meeting Gordon Lightfoot and Urban Legends

At the end of one of my working stints in Yellowknife, I was waiting at the airport for the next flight south, and I looked across the room and there was Gord Lightfoot. Not being shy, I slowly walked up to him and said, "Excuse me, I would like to say hello. My name is Rob Gordon, I am from Sault Ste. Marie." Gord, stared at me for a second and then said, "Is your dad "Al Gordon?" Needless to say, I was shocked. I had met Gord as a kid, but never thought he would remember my dad. "Does he still work at the bug lab?" Wow. I was impressed. He said to say hello and then was off with his paddles and a packsack on a northern canoe trip.

When I next saw my dad, I recounted my small adventure. My dad in turn recounted his tale of how he met Gord when he was just getting started way back in 1964. My father, who was a young scientist working for the Ministry of Natural Resources, embarked with a few friends to hold a folk festival. The folk festival was to be called the Algoma Folk Festival. The

Algoma Folk Festival Button, 1964

festival was to be held down in a small local park called Bellevue Park. As a two-year-old, I certainly was not aware of the concert, despite being held in my mother's arms during the show. As I grew older, I heard about the show. In our basement, I found a box half full of buttons. These were like a treasure find and I used to play with these all the time. The buttons had the Mishepishu drawing on them. The Mishepishu is from a first Nation legend. It exists, painted on a rock cliff face on Lake Superior about 2 hours north of Sault Ste. Marie. It has lasted 400 years and is still visible today. In addition, I later found some old posters with billboard pictures of the artists that played at the folk festival. Each poster carried the Mishepishu on the top.

Algoma Folk Festival Poster, 1964

My dad told me that the artists attending the show were Bonnie Dobson, the Travelers, Alan Mills, Jean Carignan, the Chanteclairs and Alanis Obomsawin and a young and upcoming artist named Gord Lightfoot. As I grew older, I heard how after the final show there was a big party back at our house and that Gord Lightfoot had sat playing guitar on these very stools. My dad said that the party was a wild one and went on all night. Whenever Gord came back to town, my dad would get backstage passes and drag me back to meet him throughout the early '70s.

So years later after meeting Gord in the airport, I reflected on how he seemed to have such fond memories of that early party. Then in 2008, my brother said he got a call from a friend of his who had been driving across Saskatchewan while listening to CBC. The friend relayed that he pulled over to hear the interview with Beverlie Sammons of the Chanteclairs, who had been at the folk festival and had been recounting the memories of the great party at Al Gordon's house in Sault Ste. Marie.

Beverlie Sammons of the Chateclairs partying at 131
Meadow Park, Sault Ste Marie. After the concert.

Gord Lightfoot singing at party in Sault Ste. Marie

My brother's friend said that he had to pull over to listen to the story because he was in shock! She relayed that it was at four in the morning that a group of revelers had decided to go back to Bellevue Park to visit the buffaloes that they had not had time to see earlier that day. She related that a light misty rain was falling. After the visit to the park, it was off to the airport to catch a flight. On the radio, Beverlie said that it was there in Bellevue Park that Gordon Lightfoot said he was inspired to write down some lyrics to a song. A song that would become one of his most famous songs, "In the Early Morning Rain." Beverlie (Sammons) Robertson provides her recollection at http://www.mouthbow.org/early.html

In 2009, I drove home to the Sault to see two concerts, the first on Friday night was Neil Young, the second on the Saturday night was Gordon Lightfoot. My dad once again had been given some backstage passes. After a fabulous show, we stepped backstage to meet Mr. Lightfoot. Dan Nystedt and my sister Valerie came out and asked Gord Lightfoot if he remembered where he wrote "Early Morning Rain." Gord thought for a moment and said that he wasn't really sure where he might have written that song as he had written songs all over the place in the '60s.

Some of the revelers getting on the plane to leave Sault Ste Marie. Gord Lightfoot with sunglasses. Beverlie Sammons below Lightfoot. Photo by; Alan Gordon

Backstage with Gordon Lightfoot, Essar Center, Sault Ste. Marie, 2009 Left to right: Al Gordon, Gord Lightfoot, Andrew and Rob Gordon. Photo credit; Donna Hopper

Dan Nystedt, Alan Gordon and Gord Lightfoot share a laugh. Photo credit; Donna Hopper

So it remains an urban legend that Gordon Lightfoot wrote "Early Morning Rain" after attending an all-night party at the Gordon house in Sault Ste. Marie, 1964.

Early Mornin' Rain, ©1964 by Gordon Lightfoot

In the early mornin' rain with a dollar in my hand
With an aching in my heart and my pockets full of sand
I'm a long way from home and I miss my loved ones so
In the early mornin' rain with no place to go

Out on runway number nine, big seven-o-seven set to go
But I'm stuck here in the grass where the cold wind blows
Now the liquor tasted good and the women all were fast
Well now there she goes my friend, well she's rolling down at last

Hear the mighty engines roar, see the silver bird on high
She's away and westward bound, far above the clouds she'll fly
Where the mornin' rain don't fall and the sun always shines
She'll be flying o'er my home in about three hours time

This old airport's got me down, it's no earthly good to me
'Cause I'm stuck here on the ground, as cold and drunk as I can be
You can't jump a jet plane like you can a freight train
So I'd best be on my way in the early mornin' rain

You can't jump a jet plane, like you can a freight train
So I'd best be on my way in the early mornin' rain

How an Engineer Tests the Strength of a Tree

This story steps back in time a bit. I had just finished my third year at Queen's. It was a great year at school. Thanks to a few good summers under my belt, I was afforded the opportunity to work during the summer again in British Columbia for Anaconda Canada Exploration. The project this year was going to be in North Western British Columbia, just inside the Canadian border about halfway up the panhandle of Alaska. I was going to be stationed at Johnny Mountain on the Iskut River. However, like most summers, the start of the exploration season was delayed due to the mountainous location of the program and a large amount of snow in the camp area that had not melted. I would have to wait about a month.

At the time, in 1984, my brother Andrew was living in Fairbanks, Alaska, working on his PhD in forestry and said I could hang out with him for the month while I waited for the snow to melt at the exploration camp. Anaconda was fine with that as the flight cost was similar to get me to the camp from Fairbanks. At the beginning of May 1984, I flew to visit Andrew in Alaska. The climate there in May was a pleasant surprise. In the central area near Fairbanks, the weather was typically warm with the temperature going up to 80°F in the day. The days were also getting long with light until 11:00 p.m., thanks to the midnight sun.

While in Alaska, Andrew included me in most of his social functions and activities, which seemed to be many. One sunny Saturday, Andrew informed me that he had been invited to the dean's house to celebrate the graduation of a bunch of students and a going-away party for some others. He told me that I could come, but that I was to behave myself, keep a low profile, and don't pull any of my engineering antics for which I had become known. I told him to relax and quit hassling me.

Shortly after breakfast, one of Andrew's hippie friends showed up, and soon, the kitchen was full of smoke. Andrew had gone to the store to pick up some wine, so he was unaware that his younger brother was being exposed to dangerous secondhand smoke. When Andrew returned, he was in a big rush and just wanted to get to the party. We piled into a couple of cars and headed off to the afternoon soiree.

When we arrived, I noticed that the house was built on a steep slope. So steep was the slope that the entranceway was essentially a bridge, which spanned a gap from the road over to the third floor of the house. From the entranceway, there were stairs that led down to the left and into the kitchen. Straight ahead was the study and to the right was a bedroom. There were people everywhere, and soon, my brother was lost in the crowd, yammering his good-byes to friends and colleagues.

I wandered down the stairs to the bottom level, found the fridge and the imported beer, and guzzled one down. I then opened another for my sipping and proceeded outside. Here, there was a large circle with people sitting and talking. A few people had guitars and were playing and singing. I looked up at the front of the house. It was a very tall and impressive house. On the third floor, there was a balcony where a group of Andrew's friends that I knew were gathered, so I drank my beer and headed up there. When I reached the top, there was a moderate-sized group of people talking and sharing jokes. I saw Andrew's friend, a fellow named Jock, and I went over to say hello. We leaned over the railing and looked out into the tops of the trees as we chatted. The forest was mostly made up of birch and aspen.

Upon some reflection, I commented to Jock that I thought it was possible to jump over to the closest tree, which was just out of arms reach at a distance of six feet from the railing. "The tree will simply bend over to the ground and then I can step off." Jock thought that the idea was preposterous and laughed at the thought. I then climbed up on the railing and leaned out to demonstrate just how close that tree was. This caused some commotion and a crowd came over to the end of the balcony. Jock proceeded to explain my plan, and pretty well, everyone in unison yelled for me not to do it. At which point, I exclaimed, "Of course, I would not do that, one needs to know the strength of the given tree prior to jumping." I climbed off the railing and the crowd and conversations went back to where they had been. I took a hard look at the distance I needed to jump and was convinced my plan would work.

I decided to go and grab another beer and casually check the bottom of the tree so as not to raise such a ruckus before my great leap. Down at the bottom of the house again, I went up to the tree, which was about eight inches around, and kicked it. I looked up. The tree was completely without branches all the way up to the third-floor balcony. It seemed like a strong tree. *Hmm,* I thought, *perhaps if I climbed the tree, I could really test its strength.* It was pretty easy going to shinny up the tree, and in no time, I was a good twenty feet high. Just a few more feet and I would be level with the balcony. I climbed a bit higher and found myself among some branches and invisible to the crowd that was still on the balcony. They were so engrossed in their conversations that they did not notice me.

With no further adieu, I yelled out to Jock. "Hey, Jock!" The whole crowd looked over at once. As their eyes all fell upon me, I could tell they were in shock. I had a brief smile on my face, much like the grin of a magician who has just performed an excellent trick. Then, without warning and rather suddenly, I heard a quick and sharp "cruck" sound. Maybe it was a CRACK! Suddenly, my smile turned to fear. I noticed the eyes of the balcony crowd had turned to horror. I noticed they were a bit farther away than they had been the previous second. I was now moving away from the balcony, holding on to the three-inch thick tree for dear life. I recall my movement was slow at first, but then it became rather rapid. Surely I would die. Whack was the next sound I heard before darkness enclosed me.

When I awoke, I was staring up at the tops of the trees and seeing the blue sky above. Close to fifty people had encircled me as I lay on the ground. All faces expressed extreme concern. I was feeling numb when Jock appeared and said, "It was a big old tree you hit on the way down that saved your life." My body felt numb. After every pretty girl in the party expressed much concern, I managed to get up. A little later, I hobbled over to the fridge. My brother appeared just as I was grabbing another beer and had a very disapproving look on his face. "Didn't I tell you to behave?" Jock was happy I was alive. "Hey, Jock, it was a good thing I was smart enough to test the strength of that tree before I jumped over to it, eh?"

The next day I was completely stiff with a black bruise from my right shoulder down across the left of my lower back and petering out by the time it got to my foot. The next week, I was off to British Columbia for another summer of adventure in exploration.

But before I left, I picked up a copy of *Alaska Bear Stories* from the checkout stand at the local grocery store. I wanted to be partially acclimatized to a camp that was going to be situated in the middle of grizzly country.

Porcupine Quills

Have you ever come across a dead animal lying on the road and wondered what to do? In fact, that question has been used on a number of personality tests through the years to help categorize your colleagues at work or improve management teams relationships via Myers Briggs testing. I remember answering a question that went something like: "If you come across a dead animal on the road, you...

A: drive over it
B: drive around it
C: call the police to make it known that it is a travel hazard
D: stop and move it to the side of the road

I believe I answered "D. stop and move it to the side of the road." No doubt, I was negatively impacted as I strove to achieve management status, but hey, that's what I would do. I remember once as a child, I had been with my father when the Algonquin Park gate authority had asked him if he would finish off a bear that had been hit just outside of the park. When we arrived at the scene, the bear had already expired, so we got some shovels and pushed it to the side of the road. That was my only prior knowledge of such things, but I did remember that on several occasions, my father would stop and move the dead animal to the side of the road. I thought it was simply out of respect for other creatures. So it made sense to answer D.

Many years later, I was traveling back from a camping weekend with a friend north of Sault Ste. Marie. It was dark and we were keeping our eyes open for animals crossing the road. Hitting a large moose could prove deadly.

Suddenly, there in the middle of the road was a giant mound. It looked like a sleeping bear. I slammed on the brakes. As we got closer, I could see that it was a dead giant porcupine. The largest I had ever seen and I had seen many. It looked more like a hippopotamus than a porcupine. *Poor thing*, I thought to myself, to get that big after all those years, probably the king of the porcupines, just to be dashed dead and lying in the road. Maybe I should move it off the road like my dad always did.

So I pulled onto the shoulder and I backed up the car. When I had backed up sufficiently, I pointed the nose of the car at the animal so that the headlights were pointing at the porcupine. I then got out and searched for a big stick to push it with. I found a long stick and walked to the porcupine. Surprisingly, the first stick snapped, the porcupine was so large, and yells from the car told me my friend was impatient. I finally found a stick in the ditch that would do the trick and ran back to the porcupine. I started pushing the giant beast; it rolled and left a large bloodstain on the centerline.

Then I heard a rumble and saw some lights coming from the other side of the little knoll we were in front of. I worked furiously pushing and prodding the beast with the stick. The stick was quite small, so I didn't have much leverage. I had only managed to push it about two feet when the lights cleared the knoll. Yikes, it was not a car. It was a giant transport doing about 110 km per hour. It came flying down on my situation. Although I had moved the porcupine across the middle, the truck was coming too fast; I would have to abandon my task. I naturally ran away from the oncoming vehicle toward the side of the road, well in front of my parked car, yet still in bright lights. As the giant truck came closer and closer, it was running down the middle of the road. It had one of those fancy chrome grills that go very close to the road with bright orange running lights everywhere.

WHAM. The porcupine literally disintegrated and turned into a hailstorm of deadly quills and one inch cubes of flesh. I was completely covered with dead porcupine meat and quills. Silence took over as the truck steamed down the highway, leaving me thinking about how long it would take to get clean. Is there a moral to this story? Probably.

Now I pick A and secretly hope someone else will stop to pick up the mess.

The Darkness of Ethiopia
The Witch Doctor

1992 took me to Ethiopia for a UNDP-sponsored exploration initiative. I was the team leader for a large airborne geophysical survey. The purpose of the survey was to help initiate exploration for mining in the hopes of attracting foreign investment in Ethiopia. The scope of the project was to deliver sixteen thousand line kilometers of geophysical data. Typically, a project of this magnitude might take two to three months.

When we arrived by UN caravan to the town of Shakiso in southern Ethiopia, we were fascinated. The sights, the smells, the people, it all seemed amazing. We settled into our "compound" on the southern edge of town, close to the staging ground for the helicopter. The Russian occupation in the 1960s following the occupation of Ethiopia by the Italians had built the compound. It was quite basic and lacked many modern western comforts. The compound actually had reasonable amenities; it was just that most of them had long since stopped working. Lights, water, toilets, etc., were all temperamental at the best of times.

The weather was beautiful at first, but we had some faulty equipment and some quirky technical issues with the surveying device that became quite serious and hindered the progress of the project. After about three to four weeks of problems, we managed to solve most of our technical issues. When we were finally ready to fly, we were hit by atmospheric noise that distorted the electromagnetic signals and the data was not acceptable by the UN representative. We were therefore grounded and prevented from the collection of data. This noise was caused by very distant thunderstorms that could be thousands of miles away. The next few weeks were frustrating because the weather was perfect for carrying out airborne surveys, but contractually, we were not allowed to fly due to data specifications set out by the UN.

Helicopter Airborne geophysical survey system, Shakiso, Southern Ethiopia, 1992.

By the end of March, a period of near monsoon rains began, which were characterized by heavy rains in the morning followed by clearing skies in the afternoon, but atmospheric noise remained and the project took on an unexpected shape of its own. Instead of the eight-week planned program, at nine weeks, not only had we barely begun, there was no end in sight. The crew was very diligent for the first six weeks, but the pressure from the company to fly and the negative reaction of the UN to our progress made things frustrating. Slowly, the crew started to go local.

Other issues impacted my stay in Ethiopia and introduced new and bizarre experiences. Prior to arriving in Ethiopia where the temperature was typically in the high 80s, I had made a trip to Mont Tremblant, a ski resort north of Montreal, Quebec. It was near the end of January when it was recorded as 60 below with wind chill at the top of the mountain. It was only three days later when I arrived in Addis Ababa, the capital of Ethiopia, when I started suffering from a bronchial cold. Complicating the cold, I was starting to take antimalarial drugs to combat contracting malaria in the southern part of Ethiopia. I was taking a weekly dose of Mefloquine. Perhaps due to the cold or my poorly adjusted immune system, I had very negative reactions to the drug. If I took a dose of it on a Saturday, I would be in my bed all day Sunday in total delirium. This symptom lasted my entire stay while I was in Ethiopia.

One night, following my regular dose of Mefloquine, I slipped into my routine weekly bout of delirium. At midnight, I heard loud commotions, and I dreamed I raised my head and a black woman was staring at me. In the morning I awoke and I was feeling better. I sat on the edge of my bed and started my routine. Today, I paid the crew per diem money. I went to my hidden stash of money and counted it as I always did. I counted it again. Something was wrong. Five hundred dollars was missing. I quickly gathered the team and asked if anyone knew anything about this. No, no one knew a thing about it. I then remembered my dream; I had also heard gunshots that night as well. I walked to the guardhouse and asked about that. It was true, some people including a woman were trying to get into the compound. I walked back to my building and outside beside a tree was a black stiletto. I picked up the evidence and took it to the police.

It did not take long for the news of a theft to spread throughout the village. Within a day, the ladies from the restaurant down the street knew I had been robbed. They were quite concerned, and they suggested that I come with them to meet a special person in the west end of town that could help me.

The survey program had ground to a halt due to the torrential morning rains and the afternoon atmospheric noise. So after lunch on that April day, I planned to go with them to see this fellow who could help me get my money back. I thought we were going to talk to a detective. We rounded up a driver and the two ladies from the restaurant and I piled in the truck. There was a lot of conversation in Amheric, the local language, so I could not understand what they were saying. But the driver was quite concerned and indicated he was uncomfortable driving us. I struggled to find out from them who we were going to see. After much discourse, they informed me we were on the way to see the witch doctor.

I was stunned. What could this possibly mean? What the heck is a witch doctor? We traveled down a very long and incredibly washed out and bumpy road. It was obvious that vehicles had not been on this trail in years. When we arrived the driver, Tesfa, refused to get out of the car. He simply shook his head and said, "No, very bad." It was obvious that he was scared. The two ladies and I walked behind a house into a small dirt courtyard. A lady appeared from behind a curtain that appeared to be an entranceway into the back of the house. After much dialogue, the woman went through the curtain; she then stuck her head out and asked us to wait over by the wall on a bench. When she reappeared, there was more dialogue. and finally. one of the restaurant ladies asked if I had any money. Initially, I thought it was going to be a robbery, but when I opened my wallet, which was full of "thousands of birr" (the local currency), she reached in and took one birr. One birr was equal to approximately twenty-five cents Canadian. I was then ushered inside.

The room was dark; there was a small fire in the center and a man hunched over by the fire with a blanket over his head. I was told by a series of hand motions to sit down in front of the fire next to what appeared to be the doctor's assistant. The man then took off the blanket and revealed a very scary physique with scars and tattoos. He wore a scary-looking necklace made of what appeared to be dried-up human fingers. This guy was straight out of a *Gilligan's Island* TV episode. He asked for the money and I gave it to him. He threw it on the fire with something else and the room went poof. White smoke was everywhere. When the smoke cleared, the witch doctor stood up and grabbed my arm. He mumbled some jumbly words and walked to the corner where he grabbed a very fancy ceremonial sword. He slung it across his chest and grabbed a big spear and took me outside into the air.

It was difficult to see anything in the bright courtyard as I had been in such a dark room. Now there was a lot of chattering by the woman. Finally, one of the ladies came up to me and indicated that "apparently" he knew exactly who took the money and where they were at this very minute. He waved the sword and hopped in the truck. Tesfa was now really distressed and did not want to go anywhere. Now there was some yelling going on between the driver and the two women. As we got in the car, I realized that maybe things were getting out of hand. I did not want someone to die over this $500. But everyone in the car yelled at me that this was the right thing to do. We drove back down the long bumpy road to the village. I pleaded with everyone that it really didn't matter.

Finally after about thirty minutes, we arrived at a "hotelesque" establishment and walked in. This time, the witch doctor told the ladies to wait in the car. The witch doctor looked ominous in the little bar area with his sword and spear. He wanted a drink and so I ordered three Cokes. He demanded to see someone, and there was a lot of commotion until finally a girl came forward. She only had one stiletto on. She was wailing and screaming. After some agitated disruption, Tesfa translated that the police should be informed that she was the thief. We left. I never did get the money back.

Rob in Shakiso, Southern Ethiopia, 1992.

Spear Throwing

My stay in Ethiopia turned out in hindsight to be one of those priceless adventures that you could never even dream of happening. Many interesting events happened while I was in Ethiopia. On one occasion, while waiting for the helicopter to return, a group of local warriors came by on some sort of animal hunt. They were very interested upon discovering me in the shade of a grove of trees, tapping on a computer. After a little while, I managed to talk the group into having a spear-throwing competition. When the client, a geophysicist with the UN showed up, he thought it was ridiculous to try and orchestrate a spear throwing competition. After some discussion I talked him into participating in the competition. The prize was to be ten dollars. The whole group participated. Some of these people could throw a spear about five hundred meters. It was quite incredible. I tossed one farther than the client, but it probably only went sixty-five meters.

Spear throwing competition

Rob with the group of spear hunters, Southern Ethiopia.

Local Ethiopian hunter.

Watch What You Eat or Out of Africa

Although I was in Ethiopia a total of probably nine months, it was after the first six months where I showed signs of emaciation. Overall, I had lost a total of twenty-nine pounds. This was mostly due to bouts of dysentery and other health neglects. I was looking forward to leaving by the end of June. A friend of mine was going to meet me in Germany and then we were going to connect up with some more friends and my brother and visit Scotland. I was going to take a month or so to reacquaint myself with western ways.

On the last day, there was a party thrown for those of us that were leaving the following day. We were seated in a large circle, and all the people from the local community were there to help celebrate and to say good-bye. Patio lanterns had been placed all around the yard. It was quite late and the night was dark. I had been enjoying the local wine, which always started to taste not bad by the third glass. By the fifth bottle, it was very good, or so it seemed. The food was very exotic, and as the night went on, the music and the people seemed to blur together; it seemed more and more exotic. All that I could see were white eyes and white teeth in the darkness. All the cooks and the cook-helpers and the maid-people and the security guards had come out to the final party to wish us good-bye. Suddenly, I was being passed another bowl of food. There in front of me was a bowl of spicy red lumpy things. I stared hard to try and discern the shape or the color. I asked what it was and was informed that it was called Kit Foo. It looked like some sort of steak tartare. I politely tried to decline, but many people insisted that I try the Kit Foo. Tesfa was sitting beside me with a gigantic smile and was pointing at the Kit Foo, saying, "Yum, yum." I took a very small portion and put it in my mouth. Wow, that was the most delicious stuff I eaten in all of the six months living in Ethiopia. The bowl made it over to two people before I asked for it back and then I sat there gorging myself with Kit Foo. Mmmm, it was delicious! Yum-yum-yum-yum-yum. I tried to get an explanation of what Kit Foo was. It took me about twenty minutes to get an answer. Finally, I got a hold of one Ethiopian who could translate into English what exactly this was. Basically, Kit Foo is chopped up monkey's nuts, just like the old school rhyme! It also had some kind of red sweet-spicy sauce on it. Suddenly I felt myself growing a little weak. I passed on the bowl of Kit Foo and asked for another glass of wine and a beer!

The long flight back to Germany was pleasant. I was going to meet my friend Martin Birze at the airport in Frankfurt. I had three or four weeks lined up for holidays, and we were just going to enjoy ourselves, test out the different types of beer, and then go on and visit his relatives in Latvia before heading over to Scotland to hook up with my brother and some friends from Canada. Well, the first thing Martin and I started doing was drinking beer the instant we bumped into each other at the airport.

Martin Birze and I at the Frankfurt Airport in Germany
at 12:01 pm, The start of the next adventure.

The next thing I know, about five days of German beer later, I had regained the twenty-nine pounds that I had previously lost. It seemed like for every beer I drank, two volumes of things grew in my stomach. I started to become fearful that there was something in that Kit Foo that was not good for me. In fact, my stomach seemed to be growing like something out of *Alien*. I noticed that my belt required loosening constantly. One of the by-products of this growing stomach were increasing gas episodes, some of which required me to go outside of buildings because they were so loud, long, and incredibly stinky. But the beer in Germany was fantastic. We must have tasted fifty different types.

After three days, it was time to head to Riga, the capital of Latvia. We boarded a very strange-looking plane. It was a Soviet brand. The stewardess was a long-legged blonde with blue eyes. Martin informed me that all the women in Latvia were like that. The plane ride was relatively uneventful, but the views down the aisle and out the window were very interesting as I had never been over to the Baltic Sea before. I had a few gaseous miscues that made Martin shrivel up a bit, but the stewardess wasn't around at the time. Within the last few days, I had progressed from using a belt that I had modified with additional holes to just barely being able to do up my pants with no belt whatsoever.

When we arrived, a cousin or second cousin of Martin's picked us up at the airport. The drive down to his relative's place, like the airplane ride, was quite interesting. Some fascinating architecture and a lot of very basic square buildings were everywhere. These were evidence of the postwar Russian occupation. I got the feeling from Martin's uncle that there was a lot of resentment toward the Russians. We arrived at a nondescript tall gray building. The front doors were partially broken and in disrepair. Both Martin and I had wide eyes.

During the ride across town, I had been feeling a bit of a stomach cramp. The elevator was broken and looked like it had been that way for five years. As we started to climb the stairs with our luggage, I thought I might need to go to the bathroom, but the climb of eleven flights of stairs took that feeling away. As we walked up the stairs, Martin's uncle told us that a bit of a party had been organized and that a number of relatives were coming over to meet the Canadian relative and his friend from Canada. By the time we got to the top of the stairs, we were both dying of thirst and we wondered what Latvian beer tasted like.

When we finally arrived, we were ushered into a small apartment; there were about twelve people there. They were all very friendly and very happy to see Martin. There was not much room to stand in what appeared to be a living room. Everyone was now chattering in Latvian, including Martin. "Sveiks, sveiks, sveiks!" There appeared to be one room off the main living room and a very small kitchen off the living room as well. A card table had been set up with an assortment of snacks. These included small green picklelike objects, dry gray crackers, and some cheese. I noted that everyone was devouring the cheese, so I thought, I better muscle in. By the time I did, there were only a bunch of the pickle things and the cardboard crackers left. I put a few on my napkin and went and sat on the couch beside Martin. Everyone was looking intently at us. I loaded up a cracker with three little pickles and plunked it in my mouth. Now everyone was watching me and smiling. When the food hit my tongue, all hell started breaking loose. The taste was unbearably bad. My face started to contort, but I realized I had to just grin and bear it. I smiled through my pain and started crunching this shit that was in my mouth. It was very close to the type of food that makes you uncontrollably want to vomit. Everyone was smiling. After a long five minutes, I was clear of the first danger. But a lady who was smiling was thrusting the plate of the little green varmints at me. I politely declined. Now I desperately needed to wash it down. I nudged Martin and quietly asked him where the beer was. He shrugged and asked someone something in Latvian. Almost immediately, someone appeared with a jug of what looked like freshy. I wasn't sure whether I should drink the water of Latvia, but after Ethiopia, I thought I could handle anything.

I gulped down the drink. It was dry and dried my throat. It was sort of like cranberry that had gone off. Boom, boom, boom. I now heard the sound of the pickles hitting my stomach washed down by the sour juice. Boom, boom, boom. Like the drums in the deeps of Moria. Oh, that did not feel very good. I decided to stand up and walk to the window. BOOM, BOOM, BOOM. As I stood by the window, suddenly I felt my intestines start to bind. Martin came over to the window. As we were looking out, he commented that there was no beer here and we would have to find it somewhere else. I said, "I need a washroom and I need one right away. Be discreet, but find out where it is." He came back less than a minute later and said it was down through that door across from the couch. I said thanks and quickly rushed across the room and toward what I thought was a hallway door. My hurry to get across the room had me bumping into several people. "Sveiks, sveiks," I said as I rushed to the door. I quickly opened the door. By now, my eyes were closed in an attempt to halt any lower intestine movement.

I stepped in and shut the door. Oh, oh. The room was simply a two feet by two feet cupboard with a toilet in it. I could barely get turned around and pull my pants down. By the time I was sitting, my knees touched the door and my shoes were sticking out from under the door where there was a two-inch space. I could hear everything like I was still in the room. I bent over in pain and then said to myself I can't hold it any longer.

KAAABOOOEYYY, splatter, BOOM, PUUUUUSHHHKA. It was like you were right beside Old Faithful, the geothermal geyser in Yellowstone Park. The stink was so unbearable, and I started to cough loudly. I finished up as best as I could in the tiny closet. I looked around in desperation and saw to my relief a can of orange smelly spray, or it might have been Raid, but I didn't care. I grabbed the can and started spraying above my head; KAHHHHHH went the can as a noxious orange-white cloud of crap filled the tiny chamber combined with the stink. When the room was starting to engulf me, I knew it was time to leave.

Outside the University of Latvia, wearing Martin's cousin's glasses.

I opened the door and the crowd stepped back. I must have looked like a rock star because all the people in the room were staring at me in awe. I walked out of the chamber completely engulfed in a cloud of orange stink.

When we finally left the place, my pants could fit again. We stayed in Riga for several more days. We were arrested once for peeing in public on some hedges. That was very frightening, but generally, we had a great time. Next it was on to Scotland and a few more adventures. On returning to Canada, I needed to see a doctor to kill a giant monster that had been growing in my stomach for some time. Oh, to be home, finally, I was out of Africa, and it was out of me!

Fear of Flying

Fear of flying is something I have always felt is related to some inner touch point that is unexplainable. I have never had a fear of flying. While working in the airborne geophysical business, I frequently spent hours a day in a helicopter in various precarious positions. My first years in exploration took me to the most remote regions of British Columbia. We worked in the mountain crags and on glaciers, and our daily support was via helicopters. We were often dropped off on ledges where we had to dangle from the skids and drop down to the ground. Some of the stunts were almost from James Bond movies. Then one day, things changed; I developed a fear of flying.

It started on the return from a vacation in Mexico. One spring, our young family was flying back from a stay at family friends in Durango, Mexico. It was an early flight, leaving Guadalajara at 5:30 a.m. The flight was quiet; it was a large brand-new Airbus. The flight took off in darkness, and after thirty minutes, the sun came up. You could see for miles and miles. A low scattered cloud lay close to the ground, maybe five thousand feet. All was calm.

Then suddenly, there was a bang. The plane shook violently. People were flying everywhere. There were screams; my newborn son flew out of my wife's arms and was rapidly heading to the ceiling. I reacted quickly and just managed to grab him by the feet at the last second. I was terrified. I cinched my daughter's seatbelt tight as I felt this horrible wave come over me. I now knew what it felt like to die in a plane. My wife and I held hands; we were terrified. A moment later and all was calm. The plane carried on and just quietly hummed. We were all in shock when a whimpering steward came on the air, "Señors y señoras—" but he was cut off as the plane went into spasms again. People were screaming and crying; I huddled my family close as I just knew this was it. Then, silence. We waited. Surely it would happen again. I turned to look back and see what was going on behind us. Immediately behind us was a man slumped over, holding his face. There was blood everywhere. Above him was a giant hole in the light panel that had been made by his head flying up through the panel. His white shirt was all red on the front. Toward the back of the plane, one could hear constant loud moaning. Apparently, someone had been in the bathroom and now was trapped against the door with a broken neck. Strangely or fortunately, the rest of flight was quiet and proceeded without any signs of trouble. When we finally landed in Chicago, the plane was entered by airport rescue, all outfitted in fancy silver fireproof suits. Three people had to be removed on backboards. The flight back to Toronto was fairly scary as well. Although it was a clear blue day, the winds were fierce. It was a Fokker jet, with characteristic wings like toothpicks. There was extreme turbulence and even the steward commented that it was terrifying. We made it home, and I commented that I really hoped that I didn't have to fly again.

Within a month, duty called. I was sent to central Alaska for an airborne survey project for the State of Alaska Geological Survey. The airborne survey went well. It was the fall time, and there was a very slim chance at the project completion that I could make it home for a special family weekend if I connected with all my flights back to Toronto. The connections were tight and the weather was unknown. The only issue really was that now, not only did I have a fear of flying, I was generally paranoid.

The first flight from Anchorage to Seattle was smooth until the last fifteen minutes. As we approached Seattle, I noticed that there was a thick fog blanketing the city and the airport. The city lights had made it a bright orange color. The plane was on a long straight descent. It just kept getting lower and lower. The orange got brighter and brighter. I was terrified. I figured we would start hitting streetlights any second. Then suddenly, there was the rush of the engines increasing power followed by a slight gain in elevation, then coasting and the feeling of descent. Then it would repeat the rush of the engines to gain elevation and rise above the streetlights. I found myself pressed to the window, like the guy from the *Twilight Zone* movie, just knowing that we were all going to die. The orange was all around us.

On the ground, I was happy and felt that perhaps I could just live here in Seattle and forget about further travel. I rushed down the hall, panting, more from fear than running. I got to the gate and was happy to see the Dash 8 twin prop. I knew the trip to Vancouver was just across the water. Seattle and Vancouver are side-by-side, right? Wrong!

The plane took off and then we started to climb. My seat was on the left side of the plane, right beside the propeller, so it was quite loud. I wondered to myself what would happen if a propeller fell off and flew through the window at me. We climbed and climbed. I then scrambled to see a map in the air flight magazine. Yes, there was land between Vancouver and Seattle. There must be a mountain range. As we climbed, there was more and more noise; up and up we went. I wondered if we would require a stronger plane to break out of the earth's gravitational pull. I was starting to get scared. My face was at the window again, peering out into the blackness. Was that snow I saw?

Out of nowhere came loud sounds. Bang, bang, bang, bang. Right beside me on the outside of the plane, it felt like a giant was kicking us. Bang, bang! *What now?* I thought. This was serious. The next thing I knew, the landing lights came on. I could instantly see we were in a class 10 blizzard! Bang, bang. Big thumps by my seat, the giant was trying to get in. I tried to see out the window. I was starting to hyperventilate when suddenly the plane pitched on its end and started into a very steep dive. The banging got louder and faster. I started to freak out. I was terrified. The engines started to scream a high-pitched whistle that sounded like the noise I heard on the kamikaze planes that attacked and crashed into Pearl Harbor. Niiiiiiiiiiaaaaaaaaaaaaaahhhhhh! The plane was full of noise and everyone was rather alarmed. I was about to expire.

Then out of nowhere,there was more high-pitched screaming. It was the pilot. *Oh no*, I thought, *this is a disaster for sure.* He was yelling at the top of his lungs. "PLEASE REMAIN CALM, DO NOT BE ALARMED!" He was barely audible over the screams of the engine. I knew we were through. The lady in front of me turned and yelled at me, "What did he say?" I replied, "DO NOT BE ALARMED." She was shocked. The plane continued to dive. At that moment, I finally resigned myself to death. I knew that it would come quickly. It was going to be spruce branches, bang. Over.

Forty minutes later, we landed in Vancouver. Ahhhhhhhh. I got off the plane and scurried to catch the red-eye. I walked up to the gate and looked out the window; the usual 767 wasn't there. At the gate for the Toronto flight was a 747. I stared at this and wondered if I was in the right spot. I walked to the counter and asked when the plane would be ready. The lady said we would be boarding shortly. I commented that I have never seen a 747 on a Toronto run. She turned to me and said that it was a one-time thing for Air Canada. It was the last flight for this particular plane, and it was scheduled back in Toronto where the new owner, Air Scary Country, would take possession. I started to feel a bit uncomfortable. "Is it empty?" I inquired. "No," she replied, "it is really full, you are lucky, you got the last seat." I walked away, thinking about the last seat on the last plane. When they finally let people on, it was scary; too many people, too much carry-on baggage. I have never seen so much stuff. It took forever to jam the overhead bins with stuff. We were really very heavy. We taxied to the end of the runway and pointed east.

The plane did not do the regular rev of engines with full breaks and go. No, it started from a standstill. It started down the runway. After half the strip was used, it was maybe going one hundred kilometers per hour. My feet were in the air, trying to help us get off. I started talking rather loudly. "Up, up, UP!" The person beside me thought I was a freak. The plane used every millimeter of the runway to take off. I am sure we cleared the airport fence by two feet. Finally, we were airborne. I was happy for about a minute, then I realized we were about to enter the wicked blizzard up in the mountains. Ahhhh!

It never happened. It was a nice calm flight until somewhere over Saskatoon, the pilot came on and mentioned that on such a clear night, if everyone were to look out their left window, they would see a spectacular view. It was Halley's comet. Suddenly, as all the people on the right moved to the left, the plane swayed and buckled and tilted!

Actually, it was a fine view of Halley's comet, and when we finally landed in Toronto, on systems only, I was once again terrified, for the orange glow had engulfed Toronto as well. However, the landing was very smooth. About a week later, I saw a Discovery channel special on turbulence. The show explained just how strong planes are and that clear air turbulence can cause a plane to drop one kilometer in a matter of seconds. This was probably what happened in Mexico. The show helped me with my temporary fear of flying.

Songs and Other Writings

Traveling goes hand in hand with exploration. My travels have taken me to very remote parts of the country and the world. On these exploration missions, one can be alone for long periods. Over the years, I have found that solitude has greatly assisted the creative process. The circumstance or the time or the memory or the friends have led to bursts of creativity. I have had presence of mind to let it happen and, in quite a few cases, written thoughts and words down. Occasionally, a tune would appear in the mind that demanded some attention. With perseverance and memory, they would eventually find their way to a couple of friends of mine that over the years have provided the essential musical accompaniment to make them into campfire songs.

Eventually, I developed enough confidence to want to sing these songs in front of people. In university, where this phenomenon started, I helped form a couple of not serious bands. I was a lead singer who did not have a good sense of timing, but could carry a tune. I joined forces with several close friends including Scott Bulbrook and Pete Cottreau at Queen's to form the Random Beat and then later the Sunset Trio. We played a number of house parties and a few bars. One of the most memorable events was the farm party that had a cow in the kitchen. I am sure there is a picture of that cow somewhere. It was very funny; you could lean in the kitchen and pet a cow.

The Random Beat was full of fun; we were just barely good, but were very proud of our assortment of songs, which included Johnny Cash, the Ramones, Robert Gordon, and Gord Lightfoot's "The Wreck of the Edmund Fitzgerald" of all things.

After school was over and I had been out west and had moved back to the Guelph area, I met a friend of my brother and described my earlier endeavors at songwriting. He was impressed enough that we used to get together two nights a week to practice, and we quickly formed a band called the Clamp Heads and finally settled on Bobby Orton and the Rurals. Bobby Orton and the Rurals was named after a Yellow Pages book from the district that had "Guelph, Orton, and Rurals" on the side. We played in churches and a few barn parties, but mostly performed at campfires. At our peak we had attracted an excellent fiddle player named Marion Linton.

Random Beat plays Clarke Hall Pub, Scott Bulbrook playing lead guitar, Pete Cottreau on my left, Queen's University at Kingston, 1981.

The songs themselves have become great campfire hits up at Smoke Lake in Algonquin Park, sounding better after dark and best long after the kids are in bed. I have included the lyrics of just a few of the songs that were created while Wayne was winning Stanley Cups.

The Robert Gordon

Deep Down in the Bottom of Your Heart

Aug. 1981 Mt. Diadem, BC

I would really like to know how you feel about me now
Now that I'm a million miles away
Is it still the same? Oh, do I still remain
Deep down in the bottom of your heart

Deep down, Deep down, Deep down, Deep down
Deep down in the bottom of your heart
Is it still the same? Oh, do I still remain
Deep down in the bottom of your heart

When you up and left me, you didn't tell me why
Bet you didn't know I cried and cried
Please tell me now 'cause I can't go on
Am I? Still deep down in your heart

Refrain

Do you miss me now like you said you would
Things that you said are still not understood
Call me up now and tell me the truth
Am I still deep down in the bottom of your heart

Refrain

When I Needed You

Feb. 1983

When I needed you
You weren't there
When I called for you
You didn't hear

You were just too far away
I was beginning to lose the dreams
And all the things I thought we had
They just couldn't last

When I needed you
You weren't there
When I called for you
You didn't hear

Yet after this time and all the things we've been through
Isn't there one way. one way. one way?
Back to you

So that if I ask you to dance
Will you dance with me?
And when I want to leave
Will you leave with me?

When I take you home tonight
I will show you one more time
That my dreams can be yours too
Forever more

So that, when I need you
You'll be there
When I call for you
You will hear . . . me

Rob Gordon with Scott Bulbrook

West Wind

Aug, 1984 Iskut River, Northern BC

This song was written on a long walk back to camp after a helicopter that was supposed to pick me up failed to come because of fog. The wet drizzle was blowing from the west. During the long walk back to camp, the song had appeared, and I finally got to my tent and wrote it down.

Well, it's a west wind
That blows cold on my cheek
And it's driving me home
Back home to the east

I've been walking the creeks
And panning for dreams
I've been climbing the mountains
In shadows of peaks

But I been missing the colors
And the moneys not there
Oh, you can't look for gold
When It's frozen and cold

Well, it's a west wind
That blows cold on my cheek
And it's driving me home
Back home to the east

I've been counting the days
That the sun hasn't shone
The days that it's rained
The days till I'm gone

Refrain

But I keep working for wages
In August blizzards
Today I turned blue
To cross an ocean for you

Refrain

Rob Gordon walking back to camp, seven thousand feet. Exploring and "climbing the mountains in shadows of peaks." Johnny Mountain, Northwest British Columbia.

Fading Away

This song was written after a day of skiing in a blizzard at Marble Mountain, Newfoundland. It just popped into my head while taking a hot shower.

March 1992 NFLD

Like a rose, When it's cut from the vine
Like a sunset on the ocean
Like a dream when at morn you wake
I feel our love is fading away

Fading away, Fading away
I feel our love is fading away
Fading away, Fading away
I feel our love is fading away

Like a leaf when it turns in the fall
Like a concert in a music hall
Like a memory, that changes with time
I feel our love is just fading away

Fading away, Fading away
I feel our love is fading away
Fading away, Fading away
I feel our love is fading away

We used to love in the dead of night
We used to love in the height of day
We used to love all along our way
Now our love is just faded away

Fading away, Fading away
I feel our love is fading away
Fading away, Fading away
I feel our love is fading away

The Last Steam Train

I always liked the romance and history of a train. This came to me on a trip after driving past an old abandoned train station, broken windows, and long grass blowing in the wind was the sight.

July 1996

The train pulled in at 9am and it stood still till 1
The the engineer had the fire stoked and the conductor cried all aboard
It must have been her skirt I saw as she turned and walked away
And all I was left with was lonely on that cold November day

She must have been 19 or so there standing at the bar
Her long blonde hair was flowing and her eyes twinkled like the stars
It must have been her skirt I saw when she turned and walked away
That reminded me of lonely and a cold November day

I t was the last steam train that came through this town
That carried that girl away
She left me crying, might as well been dying
On that cold November day

She left me crying, might as well been dying
And the sound of a lonely whistle carried me away
The train was leaving, my heart was broken
Tears were falling on that cold November day

A last steam train,
Ottawa valley.

That old town is gone now, the station is all that remains
But I remember fondly the days that we used to play
Up untill the last time, when that train took my baby away
And I was left with a memory of just her skirt that day.

Bobby Orton and the Rurals at a barn dance, mid 1990's.

Evil Sue

April 83

No Car
No cloths
No date
No Shows
I got a bicycle to go downtown
But no-ones there, they don't hang around
No more

I got ten bucks in my pocket
Think I'll go out buy a suit
From Sally Ann
From Sally Ann
8 bucks left
What shall I do I might get lucky
If I call ..
Evil Sue

No Car
No cloths
No date
No Shows
I got an old guitar to try and play
But everyone just says go away ay ay ay

I'm sitting out on my porch
Trying to catch some sun
I got no friends left here
They've all gone home now
Kinda gettin bored , what shall I do
I might get lucky if I call,
Evil Sue

She's got sex
She's got drugs
A little Rock
And she rolls
She'e got the nicest legs
you seen in town
She even likes to hang arou a ouund

Were talking in my room
Now were having fun
Sweet evil Sue ooo ooo
Sweet evil sue
It's all over now what shall I do
Guess I'll have to say goodbye
to Evil Sue .. Evil Sue

No car
No cloths
No date
No shows

Close that Door

December 1991

Close that door on your heart
I'm not coming home
Close that door on your heart
I'm not coming home

We talked about our loving
Deep into the night
But all the words we seemed to say
Turned into a fight

But now I'm feeling freedom
Now I'm having fun
So close that door on your heart
I'm not coming home

Close that door on your heart
I'm not coming home
Close that door on your heart
I'm not coming home

If you ever see me
Walking down that road
Don't stop and try to say hello
I've grown so very cold

Yeah, Now I'm feeling freedom
Now I'm having fun
So close that door on your heart
I'm not coming home

Close that door on your heart
I'm not coming home
Close that door on your heart
I'm not coming home

Going My Way

May , 1992

You kissed me goodbye and I flew on back home
With tears in my eyes I drank all alone
I cried for a week I cried for a day
But now I feel better going my way
Now I feel better going my way

Going my way Going my way
Now I feel better going my way

How could you make winter so long
Summer was coming but now it is gone
But I'm in the fall And the leaves have turned brown
How could you make winter so long
How could you make winter so long

Refrain

You kissed me goodbye and I flew on back home
With tears in my eyes I drank all alone
I cried for a week I cried for a day
But now I feel better going my way
Now I feel better going my way

Leaving Home

July, 1992

G
Conductor don't take this ticket

I dont't want to go
C
But if this train leaves here today
                              G
I hope it travels slow

G
Leavin Home
I'm leavin Home
C
I always thought I'd stick around
                              G
I never thought I'd go

Now I ain't been working much
I guess I'm unemployed
So I bought a oneway ticket
To take me way up north

refrain

There is something that I miss
More than the setting sun
Its a long tall girl with a deep french kiss
She had me on the run

refrain

If I find some diamonds
If I find some gold
I'll buy a oneway ticket
To take me way back home

refrain

Blue Miners Boot

1985

There's a Blue miners boot
lying broken on the ground
His pick axe and shovel
are strewn all a round
And his dreams, his dreams
are lying in that hole
The hole he dug looking
for the mother lode

1986

Between water and land
Between two lovers
Drawing a line
Shorelines

Between you and I
Between reflections and footprints
Something so timeless
Shorelines

Between the two
Something so special
Such a perfect mold
Shorelines

Till water dries
Till mountains waste away
Everlasting
Shorelines

The following is a story written in Oct. 1998 for little children. It is meant to be read on Halloween.

The Pumpkinhead Man

Once upon a time, a long time ago, there was a deep dark forest. In that forest, there lived a man. This man had a pumpkin for a head. He was called the Pumpkinhead man. The Pumpkinhead man had a giant round orange head with a big scary smile and very sharp teeth. He looked very scary. He really wasn't scary; in fact, he was just like you or me. Inside, he was a very kind man but had been cursed when he was a little child by a witch. As a little Pumpkinhead boy, he grew long sharp scary teeth so that he could eat the leaves in the forest.

Through the forest, there was a long winding road from the city to the country. The Pumpkinhead man lived near the country because the lights from the city were so bright that they hurt his big scary eyes. The people from the farms near the edge of the forest had for a long time told the scary stories of the Pumpkinhead man. When the farm people saw him at the edge of the forest, they would run screaming, "Ahhhh, the Pumpkinhead man, run away, run away." The Pumpkinhead man would wander back into the forest and cry and cry. He cried so much that his tears became the rivers that brought water to the city for drinking and water to the country for the fields.

One day, a fair maiden from the city was walking along the road to the country. Her name was Robyn. She was almost to the country when out from behind the bushes jumped the Pumpkinhead man. "Ho lo," said the Pumpkinhead man. The fair maiden was terrified and started to scream and cry. "Ho lo," said the Pumpkinhead man. Robyn screamed for help. Just then, a little farmer boy named Sam came running down the road. "Fear not, fair maiden, fear not," said little Sam the farmer boy. "I have seen this man and he is kind, he is like you and I and it is just the people that don't know him and tell stories of him that are scary, he is not scary, he just looks scary, he is trying to say hello."

Just then, the Pumpkinhead man turned into a real man and said, "Hello. Thank you, kind boy, because of your strength, the curse has been partially lifted. I can live as a man for one year, but I will return to say hello as the

193

Pumpkinhead man once a year. That day shall be called Halloween. Fear not for when I come, I will bring you big buckets of candies and goodies so that you will forget my scary face and will always have fun on Halloween."

And so the Pumpkinhead man's head turned back into a pumpkin. He turned and with a very scary smile said, "Goooooooooodbbbbbbyyyyyyyyyyyyyy." The children waved, and when they looked down, the road was covered with candy. They picked it up and ran to tell everyone their story so that all children could enjoy Halloween and not be frightened by the Pumpkinhead man.

The pumpkinhead man

The Wayne Gretzky Section

So after all that, I thought it would be fair to at least provide some basic details about this fellow named Wayne Gretzky. Well, Wayne turned into be the best hockey player the world has ever known. Wayne was a phenomenon on the ice. He has also been a benefactor to many charitable causes throughout his life. Mostly everything you might want to find out about him is on the Internet.

Wayne and I did have a mutual friend named Steve Bodnar, who was a friend in high school, and later we went to Queen's together for a while. I talked to Steve recently at a high school reunion. Steve is now the principal at my former public school. If anything, Steve can at least corroborate the fact that I did go to school at the same time as Wayne.

Wayne was born: 01/26/1961 in Brantford, Ontario, Canada. His hockey card said he was six foot and weighed 185. He shoots left. So do I!

The year after Wayne left the Sault, I had the privilege of finding a hockey card in some candy or a cereal box. The card was rather unique in that it had orange-and-blue (Edmonton colors) around the trim, but it was a black-and-white photo. Of special interest was that Wayne was dressed as a Sault Greyhound. His record from the previous year with the Greyhounds was on the reverse. I decided to keep it to be used in the book I would eventually write.

A story that I found on the Internet explains a bit about his choice of sweater number while in the Sault. At the beginning of Wayne's junior career with Sault Ste. Marie, he wanted to wear Gordie Howe's #9, but the number was already taken by another player. The Soo's general manager, Murray "Muzz" MacPherson, wouldn't allow a player to adopt a number that someone already wore. Wayne started the season wearing #19 and then switched to #14.

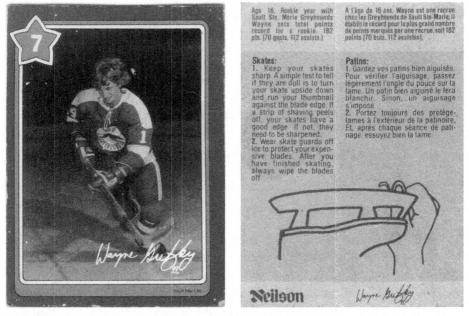

1978-9 Wayne Gretzky hockey card.

Later that season, Phil Esposito and Ken Hodge were traded to New York and began wearing #77 and #88 respectively. Shortly after this event, MacPherson suggested that Wayne switch to #99. His first night as a double-digit hockey player was a three-goal game, and the rest, as they say, is history.

Wayne displayed brilliance as a sixteen-year-old center with the Sault Ste. Marie Greyhounds of the Ontario Hockey Association. Wayne averaged nearly three points a game, compiling 70 goals and 112 assists in 64 games. He finished second in the scoring race that year with 182 points recorded in 64 games behind Bobby Smith who won the junior scoring title. In March of 1978, Wayne was presented the Emms Family Award as the OHA's Rookie of the Year and the William Hanley Trophy as the most Gentlemanly Player. The attendance at Soo games had doubled in one year.

In order for the seventeen-year-old Wayne to pursue his dream of playing professional hockey, he had to look to the World Hockey Association or wait another year. On Tuesday, June 13, 1978, Gretzky signed his first pro contract with the Indianapolis Racers of the WHA as an underage junior at age seventeen. Nelson Skalbania signed him to a seven-year personal services contract worth $1.75 million, forgoing the NHL before his junior eligibility is up. "I guess the master plan worked, the dream's come true," Gretzky said at the time. The signing eventually leads to the NHL signing underage players shortly thereafter. Two days later he signed the "Greatest" autograph in the world.

Wayne in the news the week he signs his first contract, June 1978.
Used by permission, Toronto Star.

The Indianapolis Racers are the answer to a great hockey trivia question: "What was Wayne Gretzky's first pro team?" A World Hockey Association expansion team for the 1974–75 season, the Racers won the Eastern Division championship in their second season and advanced to the WHA Semifinals in their third. By the fifth season, however, the team had passed from owner to owner, finally falling in the hands of Canadian entrepreneur Nelson Skalbania. In an attempt to keep the Racers alive in 1978, Skalbania signed highly regarded junior scoring sensation Gretzky to a personal services contract. On October 20, 1978, Wayne Gretzky scores the first goal of his professional career on a backhander in a 4–3 loss to Edmonton. After eight games, he added three goals, but the team was still swimming in a sea of red ink. On November 2 of the same year, the Racers traded center Wayne Gretzky, forward Peter Driscoll, and goalie Eddie Mio to the Edmonton Oilers for $850,000 and future considerations. The Indianapolis Racers folded shortly after that on December 15, 1978.

World Hockey Association 1974-78

Indianapolis Racers Season-By Season WHA Results

Year	GP	W	L	L	L	GF	GA	Standing	Result
1974–75	78	18	57	57	57	216	338	4th, East	Did not make playoffs
1975–76	80	35	39	39	39	245	247	1st, East l.	New England 3–4
1976–77	81	36	37	37	37	276	305	3rd, East d.	Cincinnati 4–0, l. Quebec 1–4
1977–78	80	24	51	51	51	267	353	8th, WHA	Did not make playoffs
1978–79	25	5	18	18	18	78	130		Team Folded
TOTALS	344	118	202	202	202	1082	1473		
Gretzky Career with Racers 78–79 8GP 3 goals 3 assists 6 pts 0 pim									

With the Oilers as a WHL team, he played in 72 games, scoring 43 goals and obtaining 104 points. In the playoffs, he had 10 goals and 10 assists in 13 playoff games and was named WHA Rookie of the Year by the league and in a poll of players. A year later, he improved his abilities and demonstrated brilliance in his first year in the NHL. Although a rookie in the NHL, Wayne did not officially qualify for Rookie of the Year because of his previous professional status. Later, he tied with Marcel Dionne for most points, but Dionne won the Scoring trophy because a goal was worth more than an assist and Dionne had more goals that year. That was not to slow Wayne down, and quickly, Wayne started to close on the old records and start to set new standards of excellence.

Wayne Gretzky's Career Statistics

Regular Season

Season	Team	GP	G	A	TP	PIM	+/-	PP	SH	GW	GT	Shots	Pct
1979–1980	Edmonton	79	51	86	137	21	0	13	1	6	4	284	17.96
1980–1981	Edmonton	80	55	109	164	28	41	15	4	3	2	261	21.07
1981–1982	Edmonton	80	92	120	212	26	81	18	6	12	3	369	24.93
1982–1983	Edmonton	80	71	125	196	59	60	18	6	9	0	348	20.40
1983–1984	Edmonton	74	87	118	205	39	76	20	12	11	0	324	26.85
1984–1985	Edmonton	80	73	135	208	52	98	8	11	7	2	358	20.39
1985–1986	Edmonton	80	52	163	215	46	71	11	3	6	1	350	14.86
1986–1987	Edmonton	79	62	121	183	28	70	13	7	4	0	288	21.53
1987–1988	Edmonton	64	40	109	149	24	39	9	5	3	0	211	18.96
1988–1989	Los Angeles	78	54	114	168	26	15	11	5	5	2	303	17.82
1989–1990	Los Angeles	73	40	102	142	42	8	10	4	4	1	236	16.95
1990–1991	Los Angeles	78	41	122	163	16	30	8	0	5	2	212	19.34
1991–1992	Los Angeles	74	31	90	121	34	-12	12	2	2	1	215	14.42
1992–1993	Los Angeles	45	16	49	65	6	6	0	2	1	0	141	11.35
1993–1994	Los Angeles	81	38	92	130	20	-25	14	4	0	1	233	16.31
1994–1995	Los Angeles	48	11	37	48	6	-20	3	0	1	0	142	7.75
1995–1996	Los Angeles	62	15	66	81	32	-7	5	0	2	1	144	10.42
1995–1996	St. Louis	18	8	13	21	2	-6	1	1	1	0	51	15.69
1996–1997	NY Rangers	82	25	72	97	28	12	6	0	2	1	286	8.74
1997–1998	NY Rangers	82	23	67	90	28	-11	6	0	4	2	201	11.44
1998–1999	NY Rangers	70	9	53	62	14	-23	3	0	3	1	132	6.92
NHL Totals		**1487**	**894**	**1963**	**2857**	**577**	**503**	**204**	**73**	**91**	**24**	**5089**	**17.57**

Wayne Gretzky's Career Statistics

Playoffs

Season	Team	GP	G	A	TP	PIM
1979-1980	Edmonton Oilers	3	2	1	3	0
1980-1981	Edmonton Oilers	9	7	14	21	4
1981-1982	Edmonton Oilers	5	5	7	12	8
1982-1983	Edmonton Oilers	16	12	26	38	4
1983-1984	Edmonton Oilers	19	13	22	35	12
1984-1985	Edmonton Oilers	18	17	30	47	4
1985-1986	Edmonton Oilers	10	8	11	19	2
1986-1987	Edmonton Oilers	21	5	29	34	6
1987-1988	Edmonton Oilers	19	12	31	43	16
1988-1989	Los Angeles	11	5	17	22	0
1989-1990	Los Angeles	7	3	7	10	0
1990-1991	Los Angeles	12	4	11	15	2
1991-1992	Los Angeles	6	2	5	7	2
1992-1993	Los Angeles	24	15	25	40	4
1993-1994	Los Angeles	--	--	--	--	--
1994-1995	Los Angeles	--	--	--	--	--
1995-1996	St. Louis	13	2	14	16	0
1996-1997	NY Rangers	15	10	10	20	2
1997-1998	NY Rangers	--	--	--	--	--
1998-1999	NY Rangers	--	--	--	--	--
NHL TOTAL		208	122	260	382	66

Wayne Gretzky's Regular-Season Milestones

(Career game number in parentheses)

GOALS

1	10/14/79	Edmonton vs. Vancouver (3)
100	3/7/81	Edmonton at Philadelphia (145)
200	10/9/82	Edmonton at Vancouver (242)
300	12/13/83	Edmonton at NY Islanders (350)
400	1/13/85	Edmonton at Buffalo (436)
500	11/22/86	Edmonton vs. Vancouver (575)
600	11/23/88	Los Angeles at Detroit (718)
700	1/3/91	Los Angeles at NY Islanders (886)
800	3/20/94	Los Angeles at San Jose (1116)
801	3/20/94	Los Angeles at San Jose (1116) (Ties Gordie Howe's record)
802	3/23/94	Los Angeles vs. Vancouver (1117) (Breaks Gordie Howe's record)
894	3/29/99	NY Rangers vs. NY Islanders (1479)

ASSISTS

1	10/10/79	Edmonton at Chicago (1)
100	11/7/80	Edmonton at Winnipeg (92)
200	10/18/81	Edmonton at Chicago (165)
300	3/10/82	Edmonton at Los Angeles (229)
400	1/23/83	Edmonton vs. Los Angeles (290)
500	12/17/83	Edmonton vs. Quebec (352)
600	11/29/84	Edmonton at Boston (416)
700	10/20/85	Edmonton at Los Angeles (478)
800	2/6/86	Edmonton at New Jersey (527)
900	2/12/86	Edmonton vs. Winnipeg (584)
1000	11/4/87	Edmonton vs. NY Rangers (645)
1049	2/17/88	Edmonton vs. Toronto (678) (Ties Gordie Howe's record)
1050	3/1/88	Edmonton vs. Los Angeles (681) (Breaks Gordie Howe's record)
1100	10/28/88	Los Angeles at Winnipeg (706)
1200	4/1/89	Los Angeles vs. Vancouver (774)
1300	3/17/90	Los Angeles at Boston (846)
1400	3/5/91	Los Angeles at Washington (913)
1500	3/4/92	Los Angeles at San Jose (986)
1600	11/30/93	Los Angeles vs. Winnipeg (1068)
1700	10/20/95	Los Angeles at Washington (1179)
1800	12/13/96	NY Rangers at Buffalo (1286)
1900	3/21/98	NY Rangers vs. Detroit (1404)
1962	4/12/99	NY Rangers vs. Tampa Bay (1485)

POINTS

1	10/10/79	Edmonton at Chicago (1)
100	2/24/80	Edmonton vs. Boston (61)
200	1/7/81	Edmonton vs. Washington (117)
300	4/4/81	Edmonton vs. Winnipeg (159)
400	12/27/81	Edmonton vs. Los Angeles (197)
500	3/19/82	Edmonton vs. Calgary (234)
600	12/22/82	Edmonton vs. Minnesota (274)
700	3/29/83	Edmonton at Vancouver (317)
800	12/17/83	Edmonton vs. Quebec (352)
900	3/13/84	Edmonton at Quebec (385)
1000	12/19/84	Edmonton vs. Los Angeles (424)
1100	3/17/85	Edmonton at Los Angeles (464)
1200	12/13/85	Edmonton at Winnipeg (504)
1300	3/5/86	Edmonton vs. Los Angeles (539)
1400	12/5/86	Edmonton at Pittsburgh (580)
1500	3/11/87	Edmonton vs. Detroit (620)
1600	12/22/87	Edmonton vs. Los Angeles (667)
1700	11/6/88	Los Angeles at Chicago (711)
1800	2/18/89	Los Angeles vs. Quebec (754)
1850	10/15/89	Los Angeles at Edmonton (780) (Ties Gordie Howe's record)
1851	10/15/89	Los Angeles at Edmonton (780) (Breaks Gordie Howe's record)
1900	12/10/89	Los Angeles at Quebec (803)
2000	10/26/90	Los Angeles at Winnipeg (857)
2100	2/22/91	Los Angeles at Winnipeg (908)
2200	1/10/92	Los Angeles at Washington (962)
2300	3/6/93	Los Angeles vs. Edmonton (1026)
2400	1/12/94	Los Angeles vs. Hartford (1086)
2500	4/17/95	Los Angeles at Calgary (1165)
2600	3/18/96	St. Louis at Los Angeles (1244)
2700	4/3/97	NY Rangers vs. Boston (1331)
2800	10/17/98	NY Rangers at Pittsburgh (1422)
2856	4/12/99	NY Rangers vs. Tampa Bay (1485)

During his twenty-year career, Wayne Gretzky captured sixty-one NHL scoring records. A great list of ninety nine great moments in Wayne's career can be found at www.waynegretzky.com

Wayne Gretzky Transactions

June 12, 1978	Signed as an underage free agent by Indianapolis (WHA).
November 1978	Traded to Edmonton (WHA) by Indianapolis with Eddie Mio and Peter Driscoll for cash.
June 9, 1979	Reclaimed by Edmonton as an underage junior prior to Expansion Draft, June 9, 1979. Claimed as a priority selection by Edmonton.
August 9, 1988	Traded to Los Angeles by Edmonton with Mike Krushelnyski and Marty McSorley for Jimmy Carson, Martin Gelinas, Los Angeles's first round choices in 1989 (acquired by New Jersey New Jersey elected Jason Miller), 1991 (Martin Rucinsky), and 1993 (Nick Stajduhar) Entry Drafts and 15 million in cash.
February 27, 1996	Traded to St. Louis by Los Angeles for Craig Johnson, Patrice Tardif, Roman Vopat, St. Louis's fifth round choice (Peter Hogan). 1996 Entry Draft and first round choice (Matt Zultek) in 1997 Entry Draft.
July 21, 1996	Signed as a free agent by NY Rangers.
April 18, 1999	Retired.

In 1997, I mentioned to someone that Gretzky would retire in 1999. They were totally surprised at this proposal, yet somehow I knew that 1999 would be the end. After all, who other than Gretzky would know such a thing, but the fellow who had obtained the world's greatest autograph twenty years earlier.

Earnings Comparison—Rob vs. Wayne

had been thinking of putting a yearly graph in this chapter that showed Wayne's earnings vs. mine since we met. But the draft I put together just didn't seem to give a feeling that I even existed. His line kept going up and up and up and my line was a flat line at the bottom that kept getting thinner and thinner. The following isn't that much better though. Wayne has made over 100 million dollars during his career.

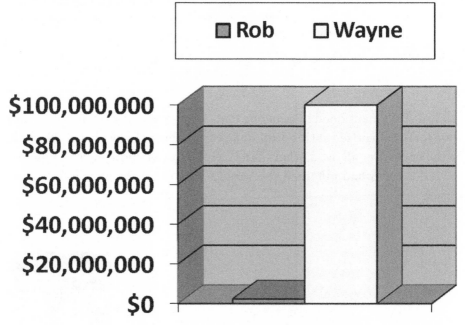

On the ice, I always feel like Yvon Cournoyer when I play hockey
which accounts for the big smile, Yellowknife, 1987.

More recently, my son has started playing hockey, and when colleagues
at work asked me to come out and play in my company's annual hockey
tournament, the PDAC-Caracle Cup, not only was I named captain (self-
proclaimed), I demanded to take the ceremonial faceoff because Miss Canada
was dropping the puck. At the end of the day, the tournament raised over
$40,000 for "Mining Matters," an educational cause, and we won! So it just
goes to show you, life is so much fun, enjoy what you do.

Rob hoists the PDAC-Caracle Cup in 2010, Miss Canada International looks on.

On Grandfathers, fathers, history and stories. Listen to their stories.

I had two grandfathers. I only actually got to meet one. When I did, it was when I was pretty young, so I didn't get to see him in his prime or listen to his stories with keen interest. Both men were in the military at one point. One was a fighter pilot in the First World War. He was my mom's dad. I can only imagine some of the stories he had simply by looking at the few pictures of him I have. It looks like despite his situations, he had a good sense of humor. I don't know the circumstances of his crashes, so I can't comment on his flying.

Yonnie Maclean crash site, WWI.

Yonnie Maclean

My other grandfather on my dad's side was in the navy. He worked on a minesweeper vessel that was tasked with sweeping up deadly submerged mines with two boats. I remember at least one horrible story he told of the sister ship hitting a mine.

William Gordon on his ship, WWI.

When he came to Canada in the 1920s, he worked as a stationary engineer and was tasked with taking care of the manufacturer's life building on Bloor Street in Toronto. Of note and adding to the urban legend of our family was that he was solely responsible for planting the lawns at the Manulife center, which to this day are often referred to as Toronto's best lawns.

March 1999

TURF &
Recreation

CANADA'S TURF AND GROUNDS MAINTENANCE AUTHORITY

Pretty as a picture
Commercial grounds the rage of Toronto

The level playing field
Lawn bowling depends on perfection

The fate of nitrogen
What happens after it's applied?

Publications
Mail Agreement
#62677

"Toronto's Best Lawns" from Turf and Recreation, 1999 used by permission

"The best bent grass lawns I found in Toronto were the greens on a Scarborough golf course." It was raised from the rough growing grass on the banks of a stream that ran right through the golf course. He left there with a number of sods in the trunk of his car and a head full of information from the greens keeper.

A horse and plow was used to plough the front lawn. The lawns were raised on a nursery behind the building over a period of two years or so, all from the rough sod brought in the trunk of his car. To finally complete the setup, he brought in mature American elms from Woodbridge that live to this day.

Innovation – moving a whole tree, 1937
Used by permission, Manulife archives.

To top off the garden, they planted royal blue violas for a visit by the king and queen in 1937.

My father is now my children's grandfather and so the story goes. He was always keen to tell stories of his adventures growing up and I remember a number of them. He lived down the street from Syl Apps, a famous hockey player in his time; he grew up in the Royal Ontario Museum

The royal visit in 1937 drives past the Lawns of Manulife place. Toronto.
Used by permission, Manulife archives.

and spent Saturday mornings with Robert Bateman, teaching kids to carve. In university, he disguised himself as a press photographer and snuck too close to get a great picture of the then-princess, Elizabeth, just before she became the queen of England. My dad has a pile of funny stories.

---

26 • UNB ALUMNI NEWS • SPRING 2002

'54

Photo: Alan Gordon

*The then-**Princess Elizabeth** at UNB on Nov. 6, 1951, four months before she became queen on the death of her father, **George VI**.*

Dr. **Alan G. Gordon** (BScF) of Sault St. Marie, Ont., was reminded on Queen Elizabeth's 50th anniversary of her accession to the throne in February of his experience as an unauthorized photographer

during her visit to UNB in November 1951, when she was still Princess Elizabeth. Dr. Gordon, then a second-year forestry student with a zest for photography, donned a trenchcoat over his red UNB jacket and armed himself with two armbands with the letters 'CP' on them. While he was trying to blend in with the Campus Police on duty that day, RCMP officers later took CP to mean Canadian Press, and considered him to be part of the press corps. However, there were strict rules in effect, and photographers were forbidden to get closer than 15 feet to the Princess or Prince Philip. In front of the Forestry Building, Dr. Gordon got so swept up in the action that he stepped within three feet of the Princess and snapped the photo at lower left. Immediately, he was lifted off his feet by two RCMP officers, who wrenched his camera away and threw him into the backseat of a car. At that point, Prince Philip, who was nearby, intervened and asked what had happened. The officers mentioned 'the press' and the distance limit. Dr. Gordon remembers that the Prince just smiled and said, "Can't you see he's just a student?" Dr. Gordon's red UNB jacket was just peeking out from beneath his trenchcoat. The Prince quietly suggested the RCMP officers return Dr. Gordon's camera, which they did. As a result, the photograph of the Princess shown here was printed in the December 1951 issue of *Alumni News*. Dr. Gordon went on to a distinguished career at the forestry centre in Sault St. Marie. He is now a retired *scientist emeritus* with the Ontario Ministry of Natural Resources.

Royal Visit 1951 Princess Elisabeth, Photo Alan Gordon

Royal Visit 1951 Prince Phillip, Photo Alan Gordon

So this completes my first book; it has been a snapshot of a few of the crazy things that have happened to me over the years. Life is truly an adventure and as you travel along the journey there is a chance for a new story everyday. The real key to a great story is the content and a segue to get them going. I have a few more stories just waiting for the right segue.

- Rob, the wedding photographer.
- An incredible ferry ride from Liverpool to Ireland.
- The amazing car adventure through Scotland.
- The mustard story.
- How to win at beer chugging competitions in China (visit www. Iwaynegretzky.com).
- The "don't trash my car" story
- Box heads
- Guy with a broken tooth
- I declare Everything.
- Bob Bell and I travel north for Christmas with Max.
- The jungle camp in Ecuador.
- The worm in the foot story.
- Playing the bagpipes in Seventh Heaven, Whistler/Blackcomb.
- The Anchor Story.
- Mama – ah, and the broken tooth

I hope I have captured some fun ones on this outing. The End for Now.

Epilogue

- The Free Sailboat

A Satisfied Mind

by R. Hayes and J. Rhodes

How many times have
You heard someone say
If I had his money
I could do things my way

But little they know
That it's so hard to find
One rich man in ten
With a satisfied mind

Once I was winning
In fortune and fame
Everything that I dreamed for
To get a start in life's game

Then suddenly it happened
I lost every dime
But I'm richer by far
With a satisfied mind

Money can't buy back
Your youth when you're old
Or a friend when you're lonely
Or a love that's grown cold

The wealthiest person
Is a pauper at times
Compared to the man
With a satisfied mind

When life has ended
And my time has run out
My friends and my loved ones
Believe there's no doubt

But there's one thing for certain
When it comes my time
I'll leave this old world
With a satisfied mind

How many times have
You heard someone say
If I had his money
I could do things my way

But little they know
That it's so hard to find
One rich man in ten
With a satisfied mind

Acknowledgment

I would like to thank all of my family including my lovely daughters Robyn and Sophie, my son Sam, who is just starting into hockey and loving it, and my lovely wife, Katie. They have put up with my old stories being told and my new stories being created. To all my friends and acquaintances, including my brother Andrew, who over the years have supplied the core pieces to some of these situations and to some who accidently ended up on the brunt but funny side of situations, thank you. Thanks to Andy Williamson for the first pass with a red pen. Thanks to my parents for giving me the key necessities: life, health, and humor. And finally, thanks to Wayne for a great autograph.

The Family; Katie, Rob, Robyn, Sophie and Sam, 2010 Scotland.

Photos

Playing the pipes at Great Bear Lake, NWT.

At the edge of the Sudan Couloir, Blackcomb

Still a Habs fan in 2008, with Sam Gordon.
(They were not winning that night.)

Rob and my Mom, Jeanne Gordon, Smoke Lake. Missed since 1983.

Playing the pipes at Blackcomb, British Columbia, while skiing down Seventh Heaven.

Leaving Smoke Lake

The Cup I won as self proclaimed champion
of the Universe...Table Top Hockey.

I am an Explorer!

Made in the USA
Las Vegas, NV
27 February 2022

44719055R00135